BE YOUR OWN BOSS
VOLUME 2

BE YOUR OWN BOSS

VOLUME 2

12 More Reasons Why You
Need To Seriously Consider
Becoming Self-Employed And
Minding Your Own Business

TIRI KUIMBAKUL

Library of Congress Control Number:		2022917683
ISBN:	Hardcover	978-1-6698-3201-0
	Softcover	978-1-6698-3202-7
	eBook	978-1-6698-3200-3

Print information available on the last page.

Rev. date: 02/15/2023

To order additional copies of this book, contact:
Xlibris
AU TFN: 1 800 844 927 (Toll Free inside Australia)
AU Local: (02) 8310 8187 (+61 2 8310 8187 from outside Australia)
www.Xlibris.com.au
Orders@Xlibris.com.au
846382

CONTENTS

Disclaimer vii

Introduction ix

Reason # 19 Escape Poverty Of The Working Class 1

Reason # 20 Empower Yourself To Be More Generous ... 15

Reason # 21 Gain Financial Education Like
Business School Does Not Teach 25

Reason # 22 Gain New Knowledge 36

Reason # 23 Gain New Skills 46

Reason # 24 Become Competitive 67

Reason # 25 Get Off The Entitlement Mentality 74

Reason # 26 Stop Survivivg And Start Living
Through Early Retirement 85

Reason # 27 Provide Better Education For Your
Children 93

Reason # 28 Beat And Ride On Inflation 102

Reason # 29 Own A Private Pipeline Into The
Economy 114

Reason # 30 Leave An Inheritance For Posterity 122

Conclusion 137

DISCLAIMER

The author is not a professional Financial Advisor, Business Advisor, Accountant, Tax Planner or Career Advisor. As such, he will not be responsible for any loss suffered by any person or persons on the purported use of the information contained in this book, even though the ideas in the book are sound as far as he is aware. Readers should seek appropriate professional advice.

INTRODUCTION

In *Be Your Own Boss* Volume 1 I discussed 18 reasons why you need to consider becoming self-employed and going into business for yourself. If you have not read the book (even if you have read it, it is always good to recap) the reasons were:

1. Jobs are scarce.

2. Jobs are not safe and secure.

3. You can earn several income types.

4. You will have multiple streams of income.

5. You will have unlimited earning potential.

6. You can achieve financial independence and freedom.

7. You gain control over time, one of your greatest resources.

8. You gain control over income, tax and life.

9. You can leverage other peoples' time and skills to get ahead.

10. You contribute to job creation.

11. You develop better money habits.

12. You make money work for you rather than you working for money.

13. You develop cost-consciousness and profit-mindedness.

14. You can realise your potential.

15. You develop your "survivor's instinct."

16. You are able to protect your assets.

17. You enjoy tax advantages available to those who are self-employed in the informal sector.

18. You enjoy tax advantages available to companies.

THE 'SECRETS OF THE RICH?'

I do not know whether you will agree with me but my observation is that most people are greedy and selfish, not only with money and material things but with knowledge and ideas that they are privileged to possess. I would say that the majority of business people are very possessive of their money-making ideas. They know many things which they are reluctant to share with others for fear that the people they share with will compete with and outdo them in the marketplace. Many are happy to share their wealth with other people but not their knowledge, ideas, and contacts.

I for one do not believe in giving people money and things; rather, I really believe in empowering people with information, knowledge, and ideas. I believe in the Chinese philosophy of feeding people for life by teaching them how to catch fish rather than feeding them for a day by giving them fish.

I believe that there is room for everyone on the planet; that there is enough money for everyone to make and live comfortably during the short stint we all have this side of eternity. The best way to empower other people to succeed in life is to share ideas and opportunities with them.

Many of the ideas I have shared in this two-volume book can be regarded as the 'secrets of the rich.' These are things rich and well-to-do people do not want you to know because they are fearful that if you know, you will also start a business and become rich like them. If they can keep you in the dark about the opportunities that are out there, they can easily influence and manipulate you for their benefit using their wealth because you are unemployed, poor, and vulnerable.

One thing I have discovered is that the world's economic system is designed to make a few people rich and the rest of us working for the rich. The rich here refers to business owners and Governments, who are really agents of the rich.

That is why the majority of the world's population lives in poverty while a small number are filthy rich. The rule of thumb used to be that 80% of the world's wealth was controlled by 20% of the world's population while 20% of the wealth was shared among 80% of the population. This has been known as one aspect of the 80:20 Rule. The 2015 *World Wealth Pyramid* however has shown that wealth distribution has become more uneven in the 21st Century, with 94% of the wealth being in the hands of 31% of the population.

The economic system is the hub of all systems of the world, and it is founded upon the concept of *scarcity*, which is that resources are limited or short. This concept – which is really an artificial creation of the people who designed the system – has been extended to ideas as well. Economics, they say, concerns itself with the efficient distribution and allocation of scarce resources but the system is inefficient in distributing resources equitably. The system produces a lot of poor and vulnerable people and a few rich and powerful people.

One of my ambitions is to empower poor and struggling people by *spilling the beans*, so to speak. I intend to openly and freely expose the secrets that have been guarded by rich people so that as many people as possible are made aware of the possibilities that are out there for them to succeed in life.

I truly desire to see the emergence of an entrepreneurial class in the country that not only makes money but also contributes to addressing the social and economic problems facing the country, such as creating and providing jobs – and hope – for the jobless and the hopeless.

The more business people we have, the better for everyone. The more millionaires we have, the better for the country. Do you know why? It is because such people create jobs and multiply wealth which benefits many other people and society at large.

Entrepreneurs *increase the size of the pie, so to speak, whereas Governments focus on cutting up the pie.* You may see wealthy people as being wealthy for themselves but if you look at the big picture, their being wealthy benefits a lot of other people, not just them and their families.

Information on the opportunities that are out there needs to be provided to the masses and not guarded by those who possess it because as long as there is a widening gap between the 'haves' and the 'have-nots,' society will become risky for everyone, particularly the 'haves.' This is the way I normally put it:

> When the existing gap between the 'haves' and the 'have-nots' widens further, the 'have-nots' will fight the 'haves' to have what the 'haves' have.

This statement may sound confusing but if you sit down and think about it, you will get what I mean. It describes the 'class war' between the rich and the poor.

I am not rich but I consider myself to be among the 'haves.' I am among the small number of people who are well-off. My aspiration is to share the knowledge, ideas and insights I have gained through study and personal experience with others who have not had the privileges I have had through my books, seminars, speeches, radio talks, newspaper articles, posts on social media, blog, website and talks on television, so that people can utilise what I share with them to better their lot in life.

The way I see it is this: If many people live better because of what I share with them, not only will they be benefitting but I will benefit as well. *"How will you benefit?"* you may ask me. My answer is this: *"The more people are busy running their businesses, making money and employing people using what I teach them, the less threat to me as a 'have' from the 'have-nots,' and therefore the more security and freedom I will have to enjoy what I have."*

Societies are safe only when the majority of people are busy working – either for others or for themselves – to sustain their livelihoods. Societies filled with ignorant, idle, unemployed, frustrated, angry, and poor people are risky and insecure places for the few successful and well-to-do people. That is why wealthy people from developing countries normally settle their families in developed countries which are relatively safe.

I am a Papua New Guinean; I was born here and I will die here. I don't want to live in a foreign country because my own country is full of poor people who pose a threat to my life and that of my wife and children. I don't want to be one of those who was born in Papua New Guinea, lives and dies in another country, and is transported back and buried in Papua New Guinea. I want to make a difference in my own country by positively impacting the lives of my country men and women in my generation as well as leave a legacy which impacts future generations.

I truly hope that you can say the same. I hope that you will tell yourself that you are going to do all that you are able to do to make your country a better place for as many people as you can influence, and in doing so, you will make the country a better place for yourself and your family and children.

By the way, this doesn't stop you from working or investing in other countries. This doesn't mean that your children cannot take advantage of better educational opportunities offshore. If opportunities exist, take them by all means. The bottom line is to make money in those countries, bring or send it back to develop your own country.

READER FEEDBACK

I have received many encouraging comments from people who have read an earlier version of Volume 1. Many unemployed people have started small businesses after reading the book. Countless others may have done the same but I have no way of knowing.

I am also aware that several employed people have resigned to start their own businesses after either reading the book or a series of articles which I published in one of the newspapers based on the book. It was not my intention to see people resigning from work to start their own businesses, but I also know that you cannot read such a book and not get challenged to do so.

In games such as rugby or basketball, a player who intercepts a ball meant for someone else usually ends up scoring points. So I can understand why people have resigned from work to become their own bosses after reading a book aimed primarily at motivating unemployed people to become self-employed.

In case you have not read Volume 1, I would encourage you to grab hold of a copy because it contains some very interesting information and life-changing ideas. You will also read my own personal story as an introduction to the book which should enable you to know that what I have presented in the book is based largely on actual personal experience. And having been self-employed for two decades now, I know from my own experience that what I have shared in the book is sound.

Be Your Own Boss Volume 2 is a continuation of the discussion on the reasons for becoming self-employed. It starts with Reason # 19 and provides 12 more reasons why you need to seriously consider becoming self-employed and minding your own business.

As I have reported, many people have testified that Volume 1 has challenged them to think seriously about starting their own small businesses, while others have told me they have already been inspired to launch out into the risky and deep waters of business.

One reader actually reported that he made K60,000 in his first venture six weeks after reading the book. He had been employed for many years as an electrician but had never seen so much money in his life after launching out on his own. After reading the book he made his first attempt at being self-employed and he landed a K60,000 contract.

He told me several months later that he was living in a new world. He likened his old life to those of the Europeans and the rest of the world who believed that the earth was flat, which caused them to fear venturing out too far in case they came to the end of the planet and fell into an endless abyss. But when Christopher Columbus sailed to America and back, he proved that the earth is round. This caused all other sailors to take long voyages and discover new worlds.

Likewise, he was living in a new world which was closed to him because the only safe and secure world he knew was that of working for others for his livelihood. Reading the book was like me having pushed him off his safety zone and into the deep sea, for which he was grateful as now he was living in a completely different world.

One lady started a customs clearing agency after reading only the back cover of Volume 1. Yes, you read right: *Not the book but just the back cover!*

I learnt about her story on *Facebook* from a post by a client of hers. When I visited her, she was very pleased to receive me. She told me that she was walking around the Port Moresby wharf one lunch time when she came across the back cover of the book. Somebody must have torn the back cover from the rest of the book and left it there. Something I had written on the cover convicted her that it was probably time for her to become her own boss.

After two years of contemplation, she resigned from her job to venture out on her own. She had been with her employer for twenty-seven years. When I visited her office, she related that business was picking up, and expressed her appreciation to me for writing such a book that changed the course of her life.

Recently she told her story to a room packed with small to business owners during a one-day seminar in Port Moresby at which I was the only speaker. She told us that she has since opened an office in the port of Lae, and was in the process of opening another office in Madang.

These are just a couple of stories I have heard. But I am pretty sure that there are many others whom the book has touched which I have yet to hear about.

So from the feedback I have been receiving so far such as the ones I have just recounted, I can confidently say that Volume 1 should have been sufficient to convince those that have read it about the great possibilities and the potential benefits of being their own bosses.

But in case it has not been convincing and persuasive enough, Volume 2 should 'put the nail to the coffin' of any doubt that business is indeed the best alternative to a paid job. It should push you and other readers into the deep end of the 'new world' of business.

ESCAPE POVERTY OF THE WORKING CLASS

E VERYONE LIVING ON the planet can be divided into three main groups:

1. The rich;

2. The working or middle class; and

3. The poor.

The definitions of 'rich' and 'poor' differ a lot but you will find these groups in every country.

Forbes Magazine, for instance, defines a rich person as someone who earns US$1 million a year, which relegates a whole lot of people to the 'poor' category. My simple definition of a rich person is one who has abundance after their basic needs are met. A poor person is someone who lacks the basic necessities of human survival – nutritious food, decent clothing, fresh water, and decent accommodation.

Whatever the definitions are, generally, you will find a lot of poor people in the so-called rich countries. You will also find a small group of very rich people in every poor country.

In some countries you will find that the majority of the population is poor, while in many countries the majority of people are working class. Rich people are usually in the minority all over the world but because they have economic power, they are the most influential politically as well as in other areas of life. Because they have more money than they need to sustain their lives, they use the extra money to engage in activities aimed at consolidating their power base and prestige in society.

Working class people can be further divided into 'white collar' and 'blue collar' workers. 'White collar' workers are those who hold office or administrative-type jobs while 'blue collar' workers are skilled people who work in factories, workshops, mines, etc. 'White collar' and 'blue collar' are terms that were used to identify workers during the Industrial Revolution. People who worked in offices wore shirts with white collars while those who worked on factory floors wore blue-collared shirts.

In Papua New Guinea it is estimated that about 40% of the population lives below the international poverty line of US$1.90 per day. That works out to around K7.00 per day or K2,555 per year. With an estimated population of nine million, over three and half million people are considered to live in extreme poverty. This is a national disgrace and an indictment on the leadership over the years, especially given that the country is resource-rich.

The number of salaried people (the working class) is around one million, which is 20% of the workforce or working-age population. The unemployment rate is therefore around 80%.

The number of rich people is very small but has increased in a last several years. Some of these people have become rich through honest hard work while others have used their political connections and public offices to become wealthy.

I don't have any actual figures but my suspicion is that many Papua New Guineans have become millionaires on the back of the Liquefied Natural Gas project, especially those who own businesses and properties in the major centres, particularly in Port Moresby. This project and others coming on stream provide the greatest opportunity for Papua New Guineans to become rich and wealthy in their lifetimes through hard work. I hope that this book contributes to the realization of that dream.

THE MAJORITY OF WORKING PEOPLE ARE BROKE

Generally, the majority of working class people all over the world live precarious lives and the bulk of them live in constant financial struggle while an increasing number slides into poverty every year. Studies in major developed countries have found that over 90% of working class people live seemingly prosperous lives during their productive years but are broke upon retirement.

In my book *Winning The Game Of Money* I made reference to best-selling author Robert Kiyosaki's description of the lifestyle of the working class as: *"Go to work; get paid; pay taxes, debts and bills; and go back to work."* Working class people generally don't save money so rarely do they invest. Pay increases prompt them to go out and borrow and consume more so that the more they earn, the more they spend and get into debt. Kiyosaki refers to this way of living as the *rat race.* It is like going around in a vicious circle and getting nowhere financially, or jogging on *financial treadmills.* Years come and go but people do not make any progress.

Working class people are the *strugglers* in the world of finance. Mr. Kiyosaki jokingly says that the word 'job' actually stands for 'Just-Over-Broke.'

In our own country, the proportion of working people living in financial struggle is probably the same, if not more. If we look around, we can see that a large number of workers do not live the lives of their dreams. They are constantly broke, living from payday to payday. As a matter of fact the majority of them are up to their necks and noses in debt. Working people in Papua New Guinea are actually one or two pay days away from bankruptcy!

How do I know this? By hearing the howls of protest and discontentment that go up when people miss just one fortnightly pay due to a technical glitch or financial problems faced by employers.

I conduct personal financial education seminars for working class people. The main one is a two-day intensive seminar titled *Seven Steps To Financial Freedom.* The seminar presents financial freedom as something all working people can achieve through seven logical steps.

Step # 2 in this seminar asks the question, '*Where are you financially?*' or '*What is your current financial position?*' We look at the personal income statement, the personal balance sheet and cash-flow in order to assess peoples' financial statuses.

This exercise usually exposes exactly where people are financially. It is truly an eye-opening exercise because most people do not realize how risky their lifestyles are until they see their financial positions on paper. Usually people realise that they have spent most of what they have earned, borrowed a lot, have little or no savings, and no assets. In other words, most people find that they have been living hand-to-mouth while many have been living beyond their means.

When I then ask how many people would be just fine if they missed one payday, not many of them put their hands up, indicating that if they missed a payday for some reason, they would not be able to maintain their lifestyles. I realize then that the majority of working people really need their jobs to subsist, and if they get laid off or terminated for some reason, they will not be able to survive. They would not only be jobless but homeless as well.

MOST WORKING PEOPLE LIVE IN POOR CONDITIONS

The other aspect of poverty facing working people is accommodation and other living conditions. Most workers in developed countries cannot afford to purchase their own homes so they live in rented accommodation all their lives.

Those who are able to buy houses do so with borrowed money and spend the rest of their working lives making mortgage payments. Many do not complete mortgage payments during their lifetimes and end up transferring their obligations to the children. In worse cases the homes are repossessed by banks and sold to people with money. So people lose their lifetime investments.

In Papua New Guinea, the majority of working people now live among squatter settlers on the fringes of the major centres because of the acute shortage of houses in the country. Not many can afford to buy their own houses due to low incomes and very high prices of houses as well as high interest rates. They cannot even build their own houses because of high prices of building materials. With 97% of land under customary ownership, the 3% of titled land is very expensive.

So working people are forced to live in settlements or untitled customary land which lack basic services such as electricity, water, sanitation and roads. They may hold *high-paying jobs* in *high class offices* but live in *low-quality houses*. Considering that they spend eight hours sleeping, eight hours resting and eight hours working, working people spend two-thirds of their lives in unhealthy living environments.

Their neighbours are usually the uneducated and the unemployed. Only a small minority of workers live well, not by working hard and earning more but by wise management and investment of their salaries in rental properties or businesses.

I have discussed the tax benefits available to people in the informal sector in Chapter 17 of Volume 1. Let me show how high income tax is one of the principal reasons why working people struggle and slide into poverty while people involved in informal businesses are comparatively well off.

Assume that someone runs an informal business ferrying passengers in a truck. A minimum net income of K250 per day is quite normal. That is net of the wages of the driver, crew, fuel, and maintenance. Assuming that the truck operates six days a week and there are 52 weeks in a year, the total income would be K250 x 6 days x 52 weeks = K78,000. Dividing that figure by 26, the equivalent fortnightly income would be K3,000. This income is free of income tax.

If we compare this with someone who works for the Government or a company, the income of K3,000 would be taxed. Based on the Tax Schedule issued by the Internal Revenue Commission effective from 1 January 2019, the base tax would be K711. This is for cases where income exceeds K2,700 per fortnight.

The marginal tax rate on the balance of K300 (i.e. K3,000 – K2,700) is 40%, so the additional tax would be K300 x 40% = K120. Total income tax would therefore be K711 + K120 = K831. The take-home income would be K3,000 – K831 = K2,169.

If the worker receives additional benefits such as housing, the monetary value would be taxed at the marginal rate too, reducing the net or take-home cash income further.

So the business person would end up with K1,000 more than the working class person earning the same amount every fortnight. The informal sector operator being financially independent and earning relatively more would enable him to improve his living standard, for instance by building or buying a house whereas the working class person would not afford to do so. The business person would actually end up making more by creating additional income streams since his time is fully in his hands unlike the office worker.

The irony is that whereas being an office worker would be an indication of someone's educational qualifications, experience and skills, the informal sector operator would normally be less educated. He may not even be educated at all. Financially, however, the worker would be worse off than the small business person because the former pays income tax while the latter doesn't.

This is the reality in Papua New Guinea. I believe it is the same elsewhere in countries where the informal sector makes up a large but unaccounted part of the economy.

GOOD HOUSING: AN INDICATOR OF LIVING STANDARDS

The ultimate indicator of good living standards is good housing. Generally, business people live better than the working class. They can afford to buy or build houses in prime locations. They can afford the banks' requirements for equity, while many are able to buy houses with cash generated from their businesses.

Again, what is interesting is that many such people are relatively under-educated. Most of them don't hold university degrees or college diplomas but they can afford to employ degree holders to work for them. Their businesses empower them to ride on the knowledge, skills and strength of the better-educated employees to become richer while the workers take home salaries which cannot even pay for good food, much less good housing.

If you are a worker reading this, it should make you mad enough to grit your teeth and give serious consideration to becoming a business person.

Talking about housing, I remember the hard times I had during the twelve years of working for the Government and several companies. I floated from house to house for the first eighteen months after leaving school. My second job came with a two-bedroom flat, but my family and I got evicted from it when the company I was working for went into receivership. Some years later we were threatened with eviction notices for several months because I was forced to resign from my fourth and last job, and we didn't have money to pay the rent.

The hardships I faced and the lessons I learnt led me to developing and delivering a *First Home Buyer's Seminar* which has inspired many working class people to purchase their own homes.

A TWO-CLASS WORLD?

High-profile American real estate investor and educator Donald J. Trump (and 45th President of the United States) and best-selling author Robert T. Kiyosaki wrote a book titled *"Why We Want You To Be Rich."* If you get a chance to buy the book, I highly recommend it because they write as rich men with great concern for working class people throughout the world.

In the book they predict that the world will eventually end up with only two groups of people: *The rich and the poor.* The working or middle class will decline in number and in some countries may even become extinct. They don't suggest that there won't be any working people at all; rather, what they foresee is a situation where the majority of working people are driven into poverty by the combined effects of stagnant incomes, high taxes, escalating costs of living, uncontrolled spending habits, and high levels of personal debt.

Such will be the situation that the number of people traditionally defined as the *middle class* will shrink and become negligible, and only the rich and poor will be the dominant classes. There will be poor people, poor working class people, rich working class people, and rich people.

Here is what it will be like if what Trump and Kiyosaki predict happens:

THE POOR
1) The Traditionally Poor
2) Poor Working People

THE RICH
1) The Traditionally Rich
2) Rich Working People

Warren Buffet, another rich man, has said this: *"If your salary is your only source of income, you are one step away from poverty."*

One short course I deliver is *Pre-Retirement Business And Investing*. The seminar is attended by people who are about to exit the work force. One myth I usually concentrate on destroying during these seminars is the idea that superannuation savings will enable people to live well during retirement and old age.

What I get people to do is to divide their superannuation fund savings by their current net income. The result of this calculation indicates how many years they will be able to maintain their pre-retirement standards of living.

For instance, if someone's net after tax income is K100,000 currently, their current lifestyle costs that much. If their super fund savings – which include their own savings plus their employer's contribution and interest earned over the years – are K800,000, it means they can maintain their pre-retirement lifestyles for only 8 years after retirement (K800,000 ÷ K100,000 = 8 years).

If they live beyond 75 years – which is most likely to be the case – they will run out of money. If they try to spread the money over a longer period, for example by transferring their funds to a Retirement Savings Account and withdrawing on a fortnightly basis, their living standards will drop immediately after they retire.

Usually retirees in Papua New Guinea slide into poverty and fade into oblivion. Many attempt to start businesses with their savings but end up losing it all. One of the main reasons for this is that they enter the business world with a working class mindset. Some gamble or give in to pressures from relatives and waste their lifetime savings. Many do not have houses either in town or in their villages so they end up homeless. Some families even break up, with the children refusing to return to their fathers' villages.

So what Trump and Kiyosaki have stated is reality in the developed world as well as in developing countries like Papua New Guinea. Working class people do end up in poverty during old age.

WHY I WANT YOU TO START YOUR OWN BUSINESS

I would like to suggest to you that apart from CEOs of multinational companies or state-owned enterprises, and the very few who are disciplined enough to save or invest while working, the majority of working people will never become rich because they will basically be working for the rich. I would like to suggest further that only those who work for themselves will increase their chances of escaping the poverty of the working class as well as becoming rich.

You know why? The answer is this: *Real money is in a business, not a job.* When you have a job, you are merely playing the game of money on the beach. Getting into business is like diving in the ocean of money.

That is why I always encourage working people to stop living beyond their means, save money and invest in their own businesses. I don't recommend that people leave their jobs to start businesses. What I advocate is for them to use their imagination and creative ability to start part-time informal businesses which they can operate during their free time while they pursue their careers, with the aim of going full-time later.

I am giving you the same advice. You owe it to yourself and your children to do it. It is in fact in your best interest to do so.

When I make the suggestion at my seminars, many people tell me that they cannot afford to save money. They ask how they can save money when they have so many expenses to meet in view of high income taxes and inflation. Some people even feel offended at the suggestion. Some don't express it verbally but I can sense from their body language that they are thinking within themselves, *"It is easy for you to say this, but you don't know all the pressures I am going through to make ends meet."*

You may be one such person who has convinced yourself in your mind that it is hard for you to take charge of your finances and start saving. You point to rising living costs as your principle reason why you think it is impossible to save. You also point to the debts you owe by which you have committed yourself to your debtors for months and even years.

I would like to quash that way of thinking by pointing this out: *If you can afford to borrow money and pay it back with interest, you can afford to save.*

Secondly, *if you examine your spending habits with all the frankness you can muster, you will definitely identify areas which you have been wasting money.* If you can distinguish between your *needs* and your *wants*, you will be surprised how much you can save by cutting all unnecessary expenses (the wants).

If you have been living *beyond* your means (which means your expenses exceed your income), make every effort to pay off all your debts and do everything possible to bring yourself to living *within* your means. Spend only what you earn as a first step.

Once you have achieved that, go a step further and live *below* your means. Living *below your means* means that you are earning more than you are spending, which also means that you are saving money regularly. Once you have savings, the next step is to *increase* your means by starting a business so that you avoid ending up as a poor working class person.

Remember this: *You will never become rich working for other people.* The only way you can become rich (apart from winning the lottery, marrying an already rich person, stealing, or dealing in drugs or other contraband) is by starting and owning a successful business.

I encourage you to start your own business just for the reason of escaping poverty. I assure you that if you start this year, several years from now you will look back and wonder why you didn't start earlier. The amount of money you make will make you forget the years of struggle. You will in fact not believe that you went through such hard times. You will forget your years of financial famine.

TWO TYPES OF MONEY PROBLEMS

There are two types of money problems people face. The first problem is that of *too little money* and the other is *too much money*.

Most people grapple with the first problem all their lives. Lack of money affects their hearts and weighs them down. This is the problem of the poor and the working class. They have too many needs and too little money so they struggle to make ends meet.

For successful business owners, the amount of money is often too much for them. They have more than enough for their own sustenance. Money goes to the heads of many such people, meaning that they become arrogant and abuse the poor. They also engage in unscrupulous activities, gamble, drink, etc.

Generally, too much money is a better problem than too little money. Business is where the problem of too much money exists. If you have been grappling with too little money, you need to deliver yourself from that problem by starting your own business.

EMPOWER YOURSELF TO BE MORE GENEROUS

WHEN IT COMES to giving and generosity, business people are generally more generous than people who work for others. Even if they are not so generous, at least they have the means to be more liberal.

Most people think business people are selfish and greedy. True, there are people like that all over the world that are very stingy. They have a lot but give little or nothing. Many focus on getting more. The more they have, the more they want. And they will go to all lengths to get what they want. We read of already rich people like politicians and business people getting involved in all kinds of scams involving millions of public funds as well as other people like stock market traders getting caught in 'insider trading' deals aimed at getting more for themselves.

Some business people are kind and generous when they have little but become greedy when they become rich. They use their exalted status in life to suppress other people and go on spending sprees to pamper their egos. Men divorce the wives with whom they started the businesses with to flirt with other women, or marry several of them. This has created a stereotype of businessmen in Papua New Guinea as corrupt, polygamous, immoral, greedy, and selfish.

MOST BUSINESS PEOPLE ARE BIG GIVERS

But in my experience, the majority of business people are generally very generous. They are big givers, and they are honest and live by high moral principles too. When they give, the amounts are huge compared to the working class and poor.

Have you noticed that too? Have you wondered why this is so? Why do business people give more than others? The reason is very simple: *Because they have more.* They have more, so they give more. And they give more because they can afford to do so. The way I put it is this: *Business people have deep pockets, big hearts, and strong hands.*

People look at the amounts which business people give compared to the employed, and say that so-and-so gave such-and-such amounts. But what people do not see is *the thinking or mindset behind the giving.* Self-employed and business people have systems in place through which they know that they will make money to recoup what they give. They give knowing that what they give will be replaced by their systems so that they will have more even after giving.

Salaried people on the other hand give with a lot of pain in their heads and hearts knowing that they will have to labour to replace what they have given – or borrowed to give – as is the case for a lot of them.

Recently I talked with a friend who runs his own business. He related to me that when he started his business, he kept to himself so much so that his relatives and tribesmen gossiped a lot about him. They called him a "white man," 'China man,' 'a man from his wife's tribe,' 'stingy,' 'money face,' etc. They placed such labels on him because he did not involve himself with community issues, most of which would mean him spending or rather wasting money on outdated and unfruitful cultural activities. He was determined to grow his business and knew that if he opened up too soon, people would distract him by placing too many unreasonable demands on him. So he refused to submit to the fear of their criticism.

Today he is a successful businessman. The people in the community love him and sing his praises because he is now a very liberal giver. When something happens in his community, he takes the lead in sorting problems with his vehicles, employees, money and connections.

The funny thing is: *The people who sing his praises are the same people who used to criticize him when he was starting his business!* Suddenly their gossiping and name-calling has changed to songs of praise.

He told me recently that now he can afford to give because he has a system in place through which he makes a lot of money. He can therefore give without feeling any pinch in his hip pocket, so to speak.

Salaried people on the other hand are limited to the salaries they receive from their employers. Both their potential to give as well as their actual giving is limited. When they give, they always do it under the fear of not having enough for themselves. The question that immediately pops in their minds is, "*What about my own needs?*"

Because giving involves parting with something they have, they think more about their own needs than the needs of the others they are giving to. So they give with heavy hearts, not cheerfully. Giving becomes a burden to such people.

Let me add here that church goers face this dilemma when it comes to giving of their tithes and offerings. On the one hand they would like to obey God and give 10% of their net income plus additional offerings, but on the other their needs are greater than the total income from their salaries. Most people therefore give priority to meeting their own needs and neglect their churches.

That is why most churches struggle financially and most church workers are not looked after well, resulting in the pastors getting involved in other activities to feed their families and cater for their other needs. They don't give quality time to prayer and studying the Word of God. They then preach half-baked sermons which leave the people the same as they are. The people justify their reluctance to give by saying that the church does not meet their needs, so why give? The result is that both the churches and the people live a vicious cycle of spiritual and physical struggle.

I have written several books on finance and business from a Biblical perspective to address some of these issues in the church. The books are aimed at empowering Christians to both manage and multiply the money they earn through saving and investing in businesses, property, stocks, etc. In this way they make money serve them while they serve God. They can give generously without worrying about their own sustenance because they have systems which generate cash on a continual basis.

Some people are very stingy. They are good at getting but do not give. But most of us are naturally generous.

We want to give to meet other peoples' needs. We want to give back to society. We want to be a blessing. We want the world to be a better place because we have been around.

But our giving is limited by what we have (or don't have). How can you give if you don't have? And how can you give more if you don't have enough or are constantly struggling with your own daily survival? You would like to give more but cannot because you don't have enough to give more. If you had more, you would give more.

That is why I am recommending that we all own businesses so that we can make money and give to various causes to our hearts' content.

MANY PEOPLE ARE PHILANTHROPHISTS AFTER BECOMING RICH THROUGH OWNING BUSINESSES

There are many other people in the world who have become so rich through minding their own businesses that they now spend their lives looking for and satisfying the needs of the rest of society. They have created wealth through starting and owning businesses and now they are sharing the wealth through *philanthropy*, which is the technical term for acts of charity and giving.

Many millionaires and billionaires have established charitable foundations for the purpose of giving which are run separately from their businesses by independent trustees. Warren Buffet – the most successful stock market investor of the world and one the richest man in the world – gave over US$3.7 billion to charity recently, the bulk of it to the Bill and Melinda Gates Foundation. He has also organized his will so that his personal wealth will be given away to different charity organizations when he dies.

More and more people are becoming wealthy beyond their imaginations in the Information Age. High school students in America and Australia as well as many other parts of the world are becoming rich beyond their wildest dreams by developing computer software or creating businesses on the Internet.

Children of rich people are inheriting wealth like their parents didn't see when they were children. Many such children are becoming spoilt because their parents have showered them with all kinds of goodies and are contracting what psychologists have termed "*affluenza*." This is not a disease but a problem which children of the rich face with handling wealth and affluence. Affluenza drives such kids towards drugs, alcohol, wild parties, drink-driving, sex orgies, Eastern religions, etc in their search for real satisfaction and a sense of purpose in life.

But the good thing is that many rich people are sharing their wealth after coming to realise that they are not taking a cent from all the money they have in their names to the grave. They are realising what the Bible has been saying for centuries: *We came into the world with nothing and are leaving in the same manner.*

Many rich people realize that they cannot take one cent out of the world. They have spent the earlier part of their lives creating and multiplying wealth, only to give it away to a needy world. In this way they become a blessing to society and humankind. They leave the world a better place than they found it. They leave legacies.

YOU COULD GIVE MORE BY HAVING YOUR OWN BUSINESS

Isn't the joy and satisfaction of being able to give generously another reason why you need to have your own business? Think of all the needs that are in your family, community, the country and the world at large. Imagine how better off your church would be financially if you were in business. Think of how many children or young people you could help to educate by paying their fees through your business. Think about how you could help a local charity organization if you had a business. And think of the changes you could bring to your community if you had the money to do so.

I am assuming that you are a good person. I am also assuming that you would give more if you had enough. I am proposing that a business can empower you to be the generous and liberal person you are or desire to be.

TO GIVE IS WHY WE ARE GIVEN

One idea I must share with you here is this: *When we were born, we entered the world naked, empty-handed and empty-headed.* When we die, we will leave the world the same way: *Naked, empty-handed and empty-headed.* That is the bottom line as far as life on earth is concerned.

What we need to realize is that all that we have has been given to us by our Creator who is the source of everything. He has given us material things to enjoy life on earth with, but more importantly to share with other people. He has blessed us to be a blessing; He has given us so we can be givers. He has directed things to us so that we can become channels of His blessings to our relatives, communities, our country and the world.

It is my firm belief that that you can become a greater blessing by being in business. A business is a platform which gives you greater ability to multiply what you have been blessed with (talents, knowledge, skill, money etc.), so that through your generosity you can multiply and amplify your impact on society.

TO OWN A BUSINESS IS A PRIVILEGE

I am sure that you will be one of those that starts your own business as a result of reading this book. So I would like to address you as a business owner in closing this Chapter.

My encouragement is this: Do not focus on accumulating money and material things to pamper yourself and your immediate family. Think about everybody else in the community.

What can you do for them? Can you build a foot bridge for people in your community and surrounding tribes to cross a river? Can you build or upgrade an existing road? Can you sponsor a water supply project from the profits you make from your business? Can you initiate a mini hydro project to bring electricity into a community which has been living in the dark since time immemorial? Can you build a classroom or a library and stock it up with books or computers for the local school? Can you do these things without waiting for the Government to do them?

When you have a business and you start making money, think about how your business can become a blessing to the rest of society. Don't allow greed and selfishness to get a hold of you so much so that you think about accumulating more and more. Remember that a business empowers you to become a more generous person.

I have noticed that many business people are very generous in the beginning when their businesses are small but when they make a lot of money, for some reason they become very stingy. Don't allow this to happen to you. Don't become greedy and selfish. The only way you can overcome the twin sisters of greed and selfishness is by being generous.

Use the ideas in your head to start a business and make a lot of money but don't allow money to get into your heart! Keep it far from your head and heart. Don't waste it on unnecessary items and activities. Be willing to give it to the poor and needy; set some young people up in business – not just your own kids but some other children. Or sponsor some of them to further their education or to acquire life skills.

If you look intently into the needs of your community and country, you will realize that the bulk of them relate to money. There are a lot of needs and not enough money to meet those needs. You might feel helpless about doing something because on the one hand you see the needs and on the other you don't have the money. You wish you had excess money to help.

I am telling you that business is the way to creating excess money with which you can be generous and help a lot of other people. The potential in you to be overly generous can become operative only when you are in business. I encourage you to start your own business not just for your own survival but for the good of society at large. You have a short span of life on earth. You need to get yourself into a position where your life can impact a lot of people.

In this highly monetized world, you can maximize your impact when you have a lot of money. I am showing you where the money is – in business. Once again, I would like to remind you: *Money is in business, not a job.*

When you are in business and are making a lot of money, remember this: *The mark of a true business person is not how much money and property they have acquired and accumulated, but how many business people they have raised during their lifetime.*

If you groom and fund several people to get into business and mentor them to success, you will be a true business person. Your legacy will continue on in the people you have raised.

GAIN FINANCIAL EDUCATION LIKE BUSINESS SCHOOL DOES NOT TEACH

THERE ARE MANY educational institutions in the world offering business courses. The typical institutions are the so-called business colleges and universities offering Masters in Business Administration (MBA) degrees. Most of these institutions teach theories and principles which provide information to their students to look for jobs after they graduate while only a few teach students how to start and run their own businesses.

In Papua New Guinea, we have several Government-run colleges and a few private institutions which have the word "business" in their names. What I have found out is that these institutions do not actually teach business in the sense of showing students how to start their own businesses. They actually teach various business-related subjects which students learn to enable them to go out and look for jobs.

For instance, they teach office administration, basic book-keeping, accounting, information technology, etc. The institutions issue certificates, diplomas and degrees which graduating students use to look for jobs. Essentially, the institutions teach and prepare students to become employees of business people.

There is not one public institution that teaches students the basic skills and knowledge they need to go out and actually start their own businesses. As far as I am aware, the Human Development Institute is meeting the need to some extent with *Personal Viability* training as a foundational course. They also conduct advanced business start-up courses.

The Small To Medium Enterprise Corporation (formerly Small Business Development Corporation) runs the *Start Your Own Business* and *Manage Your Own Business* courses on an ad hoc basis. The University of Papua New Guinea and Divine Word University offer Masters in Business Administration degree programs.

Having said that, let me hasten to say that no amount of teaching, instruction, and coaching can impart knowledge and experience in business as actually starting and running a business. It is like the difference between getting a driving lesson and actually driving a car. You can learn everything about a car and how it will respond when you start the ignition, change the gear, or press the brake pedal, but that does not make you a driver. You become a driver only by driving on a busy street. Likewise, you become a business person only by starting and running a business in the real world.

Let me say here that the real world is very different from the world of text books, theories, formulas, hypotheses, assumptions, and experiments under controlled environments.

The real world is always changing. *It is dynamic.* It is a world where competition is very stiff. It is a world which takes wits and guts to survive – indeed a world where the fittest survive. It is good to learn about business in a classroom and score high test marks but to actually do it in the marketplace is a different matter altogether.

This is probably why so many businesses in the world which are managed by highly educated people have been collapsing. If you look at many of the high-profile corporate failures in the United States in the lead up to the Global Financial Crisis in 2008, you will see that well-educated people were at the helms – people who held MBAs and PhDs. They were academically qualified all right but when they were put in charge of the companies, they ran them down.

Many reasons have been advanced for this irony of highly-educated people running businesses into the ground. One which didn't receive any attention is this: *The real marketplace had changed from the one people studied about in the classroom.* In short, the learned people had stopped learning. As poet Erik Hoffer stated, "In times of change, *learners* inherit the earth, while the *learned* find themselves beautifully equipped to deal with a world that no longer exists."

An issue I have taken note of about educational institutions is this: *Most teachers and lecturers who teach business courses have never started and owned successful businesses.* They teach because it is their job. That is why such courses are usually dead, boring, and dry. There is no impartation of inspiration and aspiration into students. The result is that graduates from such schools look for jobs to manage other peoples' businesses rather than starting their own.

FURTHER EDUCATION OR BUSINESS?

I have had the privilege of being invited to speak during school graduations. During one of these speeches I spoke on the importance of self-employment. I told the audience that the current education curriculum is actually designed to ensure that 85% of students in primary and secondary schools will not make it to tertiary level. As well as that, the reality is that over 80% of the 15% who do make it into tertiary institutions will find it very difficult getting jobs after graduation.

Given this situation, I encouraged the parents of students who would not be making it into tertiary institutions under Government scholarships to consider the option of starting their children off in small business activities. I made this point after observing over the years how that many parents had been spending thousands of Kina to send their children to private colleges or to be self-sponsored students in public educational institutions.

A full year course in a college costs between K6,000 and K10,000 including accommodation and meals, sometimes even more. Parents go as far as borrowing money to sponsor their children when they drop out at Grade 12.

I suggested that instead of going ahead and doing this (because everybody else was doing it), they should pause and consider the possibility of starting their children off in small business activities with the money they were using to sponsor them for further education.

I told the parents that if they did this, by the time the other children who had gone up the educational ladder graduated and started looking for jobs, their children who had started small businesses would already be making money. Financially, these young people would be years ahead of those who have continued on to acquire tertiary qualifications.

I reasoned with the audience that all students are in school with the ultimate hope of making money, principally by getting jobs and earning salaries. But people do not really need to go to college or university to make money. Money can be made both by the educated and the uneducated, even the illiterate. The real world experience is that there are so many illiterate or semi-educated people making heaps of money while highly educated people are struggling to make ends meet.

I even suggested to the parents that if they started their children off in business, the children may one day employ their other mates who had gone to college or university.

There are many real-life examples of this. We have illiterate business people who employ university graduates to manage their companies and literally count their money. I am pretty sure that you can think of such an example right now.

Several parents came up to me later to tell me that they had never seen things like that and that they would seriously consider giving their children a chance to make a living for themselves rather than sending them off to school only to end up looking for jobs without any guarantee of finding them. I hope they followed through with this commitment.

If you are a parent reading this, I urge you to seriously consider this option. It may be the best decision you have made for your child. Starting a small project for your child instead of sending him or her off to school with the hope of him or her getting a job some day may be the best decision you make. You can spend thousands on school fees or you can invest the money on an enterprise.

Both options provide no guarantee that the child will make money. But I would propose to you that investing in a business provides a much better chance of your child making money and living a good life than going to school and competing in a market where jobs are scarce.

I have also encouraged students and other young people over the years to put their certificates aside and dirty their hands. I have seen that most Papua New Guinean young people are too proud and high-minded to do dirty work like digging drains or even making and selling ice blocks. They feel that because they have been to school, it is not fitting for them to be seen doing seemingly menial jobs. I have pointed out that such people can carry their certificates around and look for jobs and starve, or they can lay the papers down, get their hands dirty, and eat.

I am in no way forcing you or imposing my ideas on you. We live in a free country. It is only a suggestion to open your mind to the opportunities and possibilities that are out there, in case you live with a one-track mind that limits you to believing in school and a salary as the only way your children are to live.

MOST SUCCESSFUL BUSINESS PEOPLE ARE RELATIVELY UNEDUCATED

I have read many stories of financially successful people and one thing that has hit me and caused me to change the way I have looked at the world is that contrary to what is popularly believed, most successful people were failures or drop-outs as far as the education system is concerned. Some didn't make it past high school, and most have never been to university. Much of the success they have been able to achieve can be put down to old-fashioned hard work and the application of common sense in terms of financial control and management.

Prominent examples include Bill Gates, founder of Microsoft (a university drop-out), Michael Dell, founder of Dell Computers (a college drop-out), Richard Branson, founder of Virgin Airlines and many other companies (a high school drop-out), and Mark Zuckerberg, founder of Facebook (a university drop-out). There are so many similar examples all over the world, even right in Papua New Guinea.

On the other hand, as I have stated already, people who have MBAs have been at the centre of high-profile corporate scandals and the collapse of large businesses throughout the world. You would think that such people would manage the businesses properly with the result that the businesses are profitable and grow by leaps and bounds, but this is not so.

If we consider the management of our economy, we see the same trend. We see many relatively uneducated people running their private businesses successfully while Government departments and semi-Government organizations like statutory authorities and state-owned enterprises run by highly-educated people are usually operating way below par, with some even becoming liabilities to the Government and the taxpayers. Even our public universities are operating way below world standards despite the fact that they are run by the brainiest people the country has produced.

Take what has happened in the mobile telephone business. A recently privatized company like bMobile, which was in the business longer than Digicel, is struggling to keep up with its competition. Also look at state-owned companies such as PNG Power Limited and Telikom PNG Limited. They are all struggling. If it was not for continual Government budgetary support, many of these businesses would have gone bust long ago.

Consider the Government departments. Most of the secretaries and members of executive management are educated to master's level in their fields, but not many of these departments fulfill their purpose of serving the people. Financial mismanagement and abuse are rampant and white collar crime has been described by one former Prime Minister as systemic and systematic.

It seems as if the more highly educated the people are, the more lazy and disorientated, and the less productive they become! As a result, the country hasn't made much progress during its first four decades of existence as an independent nation.

BOOK KNOWLEDGE VERSUS STREET KNOWLEDGE

I would like to propose to you that real education commences after people leave the gates of educational institutions. Most of what students learn in school is theory. Students learn how various principles operate but not how to make those theories work for them. Accounting students, for instance, learn how to look after other peoples' money but not how they can set up their own accounting businesses. The same goes for lawyers, doctors, engineers, etc.

Some professionals do end up setting up their own businesses but most work for others all their lives. The more they mind other peoples' businesses, the less time they have to mind their own. The more they focus their mental energies on their employers' businesses, the less thinking they do for themselves. And the more secure the employers make them feel, the more risky they view self-employment and business.

It should be obvious by now that I am someone who believes more in street knowledge than book knowledge. Book knowledge includes what you read and learn after you leave school. Street knowledge refers to making mistakes in the process of starting and running businesses and learning from those mistakes. It is knowledge gained from 'the school of hard knocks.'

A friend of mine related to me how he failed one of his courses at Agriculture College in the 1980s. In those days such colleges gave money to students to practice starting agriculture businesses as part of their academic work. My friend and his team members were given a certain amount which they were to trade with. At the end of the year they were required to return the principal amount, and marks were to be given based on how much profit they had made.

My friend and his team planted some food in the college grounds but used most of the money to buy chickens and ducks from the college and sell them at the local market. They did this so successfully that by year end, the team made the most profit compared with their classmates.

You know what actually happened? *The lecturer failed them because their records were not in order!* The other teams received good marks because they had kept all the receipts and their books were in order as they had learnt in class, even though they had lost most of the 'seed' money. Today, this friend of mine runs his own family company which turns over several million Kina a year.

The morale of this story is that sometimes school is too fussy about paper work and doing things by the textbook. I am not saying that good records are unimportant; they are. But school forces people to go by the textbook more than to improvise and find their own ingenious way through problems. It suppresses peoples' creative and entrepreneurial ability. No wonder many academically successful people are financial failures. They can be referred to as *'A' people academically, high-fliers professionally, but 'F' people financially.*

If you forget everything in this Chapter, one thing I urge you not forget is that if you really want to learn about business, there is nothing like actually starting one and running it yourself. The sooner you start your business, the better.

If the business fails, remember that you haven't failed. In fact you have learnt some valuable lessons. What you lose is not gone forever; it is actually an investment in your education. Take the loss as a fee for the education you have received.

I myself started seven businesses. All of them failed and I lost a lot of money. But I persisted. I got up, shook the dust off, and made another attempt. I can tell you from experience that I have learnt more about business by being in business than what I learnt while studying economics at university. It will be the same with you.

Let me end with a quote from Donald J. Trump in the book *The Midas Touch* which he and Robert T. Kiyosaki co-wrote:

> A business is the best personal-development program you can get on, and it is the best business school you can enroll in.

This is true. You will never learn much about business until you establish and run one. A business helps you to discover your potential, and it provides the best opportunity to learn about business using real money, losing real money, and making real money. No amount of classroom learning or reading from books can compensate for that.

GAIN NEW KNOWLEDGE

B USINESS IS REALLY a world of its own which most people are not aware of. Even people who work in businesses are not conscious of the world they operate in. And most educated people are not aware that it exists, because they were taught to *work for* business people, not to *become* business people.

THE HIGHER YOU GO UP THE EDUCATIONAL LADDER, THE MORE YOU KNOW ABOUT LESS AND LESS

The way the education system works is that it trains people to become professionals in one area of life. The system is designed to have students start out as *generalists* and end up as *specialists*. *The higher they go up the educational ladder, the more and more they learn about less and less.*

They learn more about one area and less or little about all other areas. They earn Masters Degrees, for instance, meaning that they master or understand more fully the area they have studied. But note that it is only to a *degree*. They don't know everything about that area, and certainly not as much about many other areas.

People who continue to PhD level gain so much in-depth knowledge of their area of specialty to the exclusion of most other areas (unless they go beyond what their lecturers and supervisors require and do their own learning). That is why most highly educated people can work in an organization but they cannot start their own. They just do not possess the broad knowledge and skills to be able to put a lot of systems together to form a business or other organization.

They become so engrossed in minding their small sections and departments that they do not get a bird's eye view of the whole organization. They get so buried in the daily details that they become less aware of the 'big picture.'

EVERY FIELD IS A WORLD OF ITS OWN

Every field of expertise is a world of its own. It has its own language or terminology, laws, rules, regulations, conventions, traditions, etiquette, procedures, processes, protocols, etc.

Listen to two medical doctors conversing in English and you will think they are speaking German. Although you can hear them use English words which you may be familiar with, you cannot understand what they are saying because those words have different meanings in the medical world. Likewise, you cannot follow when lawyers or accountants are talking among themselves.

In the world of stock market investing, a 'bear' is not an animal; it is a person who thinks prices of shares will fall (so he sells the shares he has while prices are high, or refrains from buying in order to buy later when prices fall), and a 'bull' is not an animal either; it is someone who is optimistic and believes that share prices will rise (so he refrains from selling with the intention of selling when prices rise). Neither are 'pigs' and 'chickens' animals; they are people who demonstrate certain behaviors in the market. (Chickens are those who watch on the sidelines in fear while pigs jump in thoughtlessly and get slaughtered.)

Business is similar. There are terminologies and laws which define different business organizations and how such businesses are supposed and expected to be run. There are laws which govern how business owners and managers in different sectors need to conduct themselves. There are laws which govern how business owners should treat their workers. There are sections within the tax code which give business owners a lot of loopholes to minimize and even avoid taxes which are not available to workers, some of which were highlighted in Chapter 18 of Volume 1. It is, again, a world of its own.

Have you ever wondered why every newspaper has a business section? You pick up any newspaper anywhere in the world and you will not fail to find a business section. That is the first section people in the business world turn to, even before they read the headlines and other stories. Even as sports people turn to the sports section of newspapers first, business people turn to the business section. (Generally, sports people read newspapers from the back; people with political interests read from the front; and business people start in the middle).

You will notice that the language used in the business section is quite difficult to understand too. It is English all right but most of the words have different meanings to ordinary English. That is why common people skip over the business section in favour of political news and sports stories.

You will find subsections which contain exchange rates, interest rates, share prices, commodity prices, summaries of developments in major share markets in the world the day before, etc. These are all bits of information people in the business world need to know on a daily basis in order to conduct their businesses. If you look at those numbers as an ordinary person, you will not know what they mean but business people (many, not all though) know what the figures and numbers mean. They even know how to translate the information or use it to carry out calculations using formulas which are in their heads.

For instance, people in the export/import business are usually interested in the foreign currency market which might have an impact on the exchange rates they use in the course of their business transactions. People in the share market read about what happened in a particular exchange as well as how the companies whose shares they own have been faring.

Again, business is a world most common folk are not familiar with.

MONEY IS MADE THROUGH BUSINESSES, NOT JOBS

Money is truly made in the world of business. In fact, a business is a system created to make money by meeting the needs or solving the problems of society. I normally define a business as a 'money printing machine.' What employees get in the form of wages and salaries, commissions, bonuses, etc, is a little share of what businesses spin off. It is like the residue from what the business owner makes from his system. That is why I have written this book and others to encourage as many people as possible to get into business. If you want to make as much money as you can, a job will certainly not give you the opportunity; only a business can.

When you enter the business world, you will realize that there are so many things you did not know which you must know in order to survive in your new world. When you hold a job you do not feel the force of competition in the market, for instance. You are comfortable in your job. As long as you do what you are required to do, you get your pay. Your income, which is guaranteed under your employment contract, is the business owner's problem. It is like living in a lagoon.

But in business, there are no guarantees and certainties. You make money today and tomorrow you might not make any money at all. In fact, it might be the case that you don't make any money for weeks and months because competition in the business world is very stiff and tough. Your eyes as the business owner will be constantly on the 'bottom line.'

If being an employee is like living in a lagoon or on the beach, being in business can be likened to living out in the open sea.

When you get into business, you will realize that there are many responsibilities upon you as a business owner. For instance, you have to submit Annual Returns to the Investment Promotion Authority. You also have to submit Tax Returns to the Tax Office. You have to submit payroll taxes to the Tax Office. And you have to get your workers insured under the Workers Compensation Act as well as be familiar and comply with rules, policies and regulations covering the industry your business operates in.

SOME KNOWLEDGE OF ECONOMICS IS VITAL

If you have been trained as an accountant and you go into business, you will realize that some knowledge of law is necessary. If you have been trained as a lawyer, you will need to gain accounting knowledge. If you are a medical doctor going into private practice, you will need some accounting and legal knowledge to conduct your business successfully and legally. You will realize that no matter what field you have received training in, and what business you are in or intend to get into, basic knowledge of economics is vital.

Let me hasten to say here that trained economists do not know everything about how the economy operates. If they did, we would not have any problems with our economy. The fact that we have so many problems with the economy shows that economists do not really understand how it operates. This is mainly because the economy is actually the sum of the human emotions of fear, greed, and selfishness. That is why economists usually get things wrong a lot of times. They predict that the economy will grow, and it contracts instead, and so on.

Having said that, let me say also that economists do possess overall knowledge of the economy. The economy is basically made up of production, distribution, consumption, and financing systems. Economists have some understanding of how various economic variables interact with each other to make the economy what it is.

For instance, they know how employment and wages (which are part of the micro economy) impact on the country's balance of payments and exchange rates (which are part of the macro economy). They know the relationship between interest rates and the general price level in the country.

Am I saying that you cannot get into business if you are not an economist? No. What I am saying is that anybody can get into business, but in order to *succeed*, you will find it necessary to get some understanding of how the economy works because the economy is the general environment in which your business exists. You must understand how what you are doing fits into what is happening in the economy; by the same token, you must understand how what happens in the economy impacts on your business, and how you can position your business to take advantage of opportunities for growth and expansion.

For example, what will be the impact of exchange rate appreciation on business in general and your business in particular? People generally believe that a strong local currency is good for the economy, but is it good for everyone? What if you are in the export business? What happens when the exchange rate is unstable?

What will happen to your business in an economy where the cost of borrowing money rises? What is likely to happen to the interest rate if the Government increases its borrowings from the domestic financial market? Or what will happen to your business when the Government increases the company tax rate in an effort to raise money to settle its debts, or gives tax concessions to some companies?

What are the implications on businesses of an announcement by the Central Bank that it is going to pursue a 'tight' monetary policy? What happens when the rate of inflation fluctuates constantly, or the Government faces a cash-flow crisis?

These are the types of questions you will be confronted with as a business person because what happens in the economy will have a direct bearing on your business's profitability. Do you think most employees understand or even care about these economic variables? My bet is they don't. Do business people take note? I bet that most do.

BASIC ACCOUNTING KNOWLEGDE IS ALSO VITAL

While economics is important for you to understand how events taking place in the economy impact on your business, some knowledge of accounting will be essential to understand what is happening *within* your business.

Many business people have never been to accounting school so they rely totally on the advice of their accountants. This is in my view not good for them as business owners because I have seen many business people being cheated by accountants and managers because they (business owners) do not know basic accounting. There have been many instances of expatriate accountants making off with their employers' money and the local business people could not trace them and get their money back.

Some business people are given information and advice by their accountants, but they do not know how to use the information and so they make financial mistakes or allow opportunities to go by them.

You as the owner will be required to know the *cash position* and *cash flow* situation in your business. You must be able to read and understand financial statements such as the *income* or *profit and loss statement* and *balance sheet* that are prepared by your accountants.

You will be forced to know what your creditors' and debtors' position is. You will need to know the depreciation rate for capital items and the accounting method used by your accountant because that has a bearing on your profit or loss. The depreciation method and rate has tax implications as well.

SOME KNOWLEGDE OF LAW IS NECESSARY

Businesses also operate in a legal environment. There are different branches of law covering the operations of businesses, contracts and agreements between businesses, company and personal income tax, relationships between employers and employees, the environment, workplace safety and occupational health, discrimination, competition and pricing, insurance of property and personnel, workers' compensation, industrial disputes, transfer of property ownership, etc.

You will not be required to know or understand the law in order to become a business person, but you will definitely come face to face with some legal issues from the first day you open your business to the public. Most business people ignore the law or their legal obligations until they get into trouble with the law. It is only then that they start taking an interest in legal matters. Wise people however find out as much as they can about what the law says about business generally and in relation to their particular business activities. You will find this necessary as a serious business person.

My point is this: *When you get into business, you will be forced to learn things you never learnt in school.* You will be forced to become a *generalist.* You will gain new knowledge of how the business world operates. You will learn new terms and vocabulary. And the more you speak in those terms, the more people will respect you and think you are an economist, an accountant, or even a lawyer. That's cool, isn't it?

GAIN NEW SKILLS

A S I HAVE stated in the last Chapter, the business world is a world of its own. It is a tough world too because you are out there in a competitive marketplace which usually has no mercy for the complacent and the slothful. It is a world where the term 'survival of the fittest' fits nicely.

In order to play the game, survive, and thrive, you will have to both gain new knowledge and develop new skills as a business owner.

YOU WILL DEVELOP SO MANY SKILLS

You will definitely gain and develop many new skills as a business owner. If you have been to school, the skills you will learn may have been introduced to you at some stage but you did not have the opportunity to develop them further. Most people however will find that school has not prepared them at all to function in the business world because as I have mentioned several times throughout the book, schools have been introduced to produce employees, not business people and employers.

If you have not been to school, don't worry because you are on the same footing as most people who have been to school. All of you have to develop the skills necessary for marketplace survival.

Let us now consider just ten of the important skills you will need to develop as a business person.

SKILL # 1: PEOPLE

No matter how small your business may be, you will inevitably deal with people. Remember, a business exists primarily to meet peoples' needs or solve their problems. So the day you open your business is the day you start dealing with people and their problems and needs.

The first group of people you come into contact with are your *customers*. You will deal with this group of people every day of your life as a business person. Most customers will be easy to deal with, while some might be too demanding or even intimidating. You have to learn to put up with all these people as it is because of them that you exist as a business person, and they determine whether your business survives or dies.

For you as a business person, the customers are the most important people because no customer means no business. Sometimes you will realise that despite how right you are and how wrong the customers are, the cardinal law in the business world is, *the customer is always right*. Or as other people say, *the customer is king*.

In a business world that is crazily competitive, your survival depends on how you treat your customers. Mistreat them and you get hit at the 'bottom line;' welcome, respect, appreciate, and satisfy them, and your bottom line remains in the 'black.'

The other group of people you will deal with are your *employees*. You will also find all kinds of people within this group. Some join you to genuinely help you grow your business while some come just for the pay cheque. Some will be easy going and submissive while others will be hard and challenge you despite the fact that you are the owner of the business. Some will steal from you if given the chance and some may even sabotage your business.

Being in business will definitely enable you to develop a 'feel' for different kinds of people in the world and their tendencies and personalities. Over time you will be able to make distinctions between those who have impressive academic qualifications and CVs and those that are really skilled and committed. You will certainly develop your own set of skills for interviewing would-be employees as well as for discovering what makes them 'tick,' and how to motivate them to be productive.

You will also deal with your *suppliers*. They are the people and organisations from whom you obtain your raw materials. Again, some of them will be easy with you while others have no respect for you, especially if you are small or are a new client to them. It will take time for you to win their trust and confidence. Some will not apply the rule that you, their customer, are always right. You will have to develop your own unique way of dealing with such people.

You will definitely come across other members of the public and Government officials including members of the police force, some of whom will grab any opportunity to squeeze something out of you (because you are a business person and you supposedly always have a pocketful of money to hand out).

There are many other groups of people who you will have to deal with. Of them all, probably the most notorious group you have to handle as a Papua New Guinean business person are your *relatives*, tribe members, and people who come from the same area as you (your *wantoks*). You will definitely be confronted by these people with their needs and demands for cash, in-kind contributions, or employment. They will threaten to call you names (like 'penny-pincher,' 'money face,' 'white-skin,' 'Kong Kong') if you do not entertain them. Some will spread false rumours about you, or flatter and praise you in your presence but slander and curse you at your back.

I do not want to frighten you if you are not a 'people' person. Being in business and dealing with people is very rewarding. At the end of the day, you are a human being, and human beings were created to enjoy life in association with other human beings. As the popular saying goes, *"No man is an island."*

You might find that you are able to relate to people but have been thinking that you cannot. Being in business awakens your latent potential to relate to people from all walks of life. You might find that you become a better person in the process as your interaction with people shapes and molds you. They sharpen and knock you into shape, so to speak. As the Bible says, *"In the same way that iron sharpens iron, so a man sharpens the countenance of his friend."*

My point is that you will develop your own set of skills and techniques to deal with different kinds of people. You would deal with the same group of people in a certain manner being an employee, but being a business owner, your approach will certainly be different. Whatever happens, one consequence will be this: *You will grow as a person in the process of establishing and operating your own business.*

SKILL # 2: LEADERSHIP

As a business person you will find that what Harry S. Truman, 33rd President of the United States stated – '*The buck stops here.*' – applies to you. At the end of the day, you are solely responsible for the success or failure of your business. The buck stops with you.

You cannot blame your clients, employees, suppliers, the Government or others such as your spouse, children, or relatives. You will find that you are expected to *take the blame* when things do not work out, but that you have to *share the credit* when the business succeeds.

You will find that success or failure depends on your leadership more than anything else. As American leadership guru John C. Maxwell has stated, "*Everything rises or falls on leadership.*" What makes one country become powerful and another weak is the quality of their leadership, not how rich or poor the country is.

Likewise, what makes one business expand and another falter is the foresight and prudence of its leadership, not a lack of resources. Your business may make a lot of money but if you do not lead well, it won't be long before all you have made gets transferred to those who lead better than you.

Leadership is a vital skill you will learn as a business person. Not only do you have to make sure that the business succeeds and goes from strength to strength, but you have other collateral responsibilities as well. For instance, your employees and their dependents' welfare will to a large extent be determined by your leadership of the business. If the business grows, these people have a means of living; if it falters, a lot of people will suffer. It is as serious as children not being able to go to school or families not having meals to look forward to at the end of each day.

When I talk to business people I find that most of them think about the success of their businesses first and foremost in connection with the survival of their own families. This to me is a very limited view to hold. I tell them that they are not only in business for themselves but for the rest of society. Their businesses generate cashflow which gets spread around; their businesses spawn other businesses which become suppliers and customers to them; their businesses provide jobs which support many other people; their businesses provide tax income to the Government to fund development projects for the good of everybody in the country.

When you think in those terms, you will find that you, as a business person, are a leader in your own right. You are not struggling to run a business in some small corner of the country without any recognition from anyone. People may not recognise and applaud you but you are a leader for sure to the people who work for you, their dependents, and the surrounding community. Many people's lives will be positively impacted as you develop and display your leadership skills through your business.

As the leader, one of the most important roles you play will be casting the business's vision and the way forward. You started the business because you saw a need in the community and the business was your solution to those needs. For the business to survive and grow, you need to continue to look around you as well as to see into the future. You are the dreamer; and you are the carrier of the vision.

You have a 'bird's-eye' view of the economy and the business environment, while many of your employees have a 'worm's-eye' view. You have to think 'big-picture' while your employees concern themselves with the nitty-gritty's of the business. Stop dreaming and your business stagnates; continue dreaming and your business takes risks, ventures out, stays alive, and expands.

When you are an employee, you may be placed in positions of leadership as a supervisor, manager or even chief executive officer. But at the bottom of your heart, you know that the business does not belong to you. So you will not give it your best shot. You will go just far enough to maintain your benefits and even get a raise or bonus. But when you are the owner, you give the business 101% as its leader.

It is challenging and even life-changing. But you will no doubt find it a rewarding experience. It makes life exciting to live. Every good decision you make stretches you a bit more and motivates you to reach out a little bit more. Every mistake you make becomes a learning experience from which you emerge stronger and wiser. As your business grows, you grow as a person.

SKILL # 3: TEAM BUILDING AND DELEGATION

Most businesses start as one-person operations but as they grow and expand, the founders realise that they need to build a team of people with the requisite knowledge, skills, and other characteristics if their businesses are to survive in the market as well as grow further. Teams are essential for winning sporting games; likewise, to win the game of entrepreneurship and money, a good team is vital. And the team may comprise of full time employees or certain people you engage from time to time, or a combination of both.

As mentioned above, you become the leader of the enterprise, but this necessarily means that you have a team behind you or with you. In addition to developing the skill of building a winning team, you will also be forced to develop the skill of delegating responsibilities to team members that are most qualified. This will entail assessing all the strengths and weaknesses of the team.

Depending on the nature of your business, you may find that your role may change from one of leading from the front to one of coaching, guiding and mentoring from behind. In the final analysis, what matters is not who is seen to be the leader, but how the business is faring in the marketplace. Of course you as the owner have the final say but you will find that team members will make most of the day-to-day decisions.

Many businesses miss opportunities because the owners have a monopoly over even the mundane decisions. Many employees feel frustrated when they are required to defer to the owners every time a decision has to be made. Delegation is therefore definitely a skill you will be obliged to develop. Of course the employees have to win your trust but once they do and once you delegate, you also lose some power to them. This is all part of the game.

SKILL # 4: FINANCIAL MANAGEMENT

A business exists to meet needs, and gets paid in return. What the business makes is its reward for meeting the needs, solving the problems, and making life convenient for people. The more efficiently it meets needs, the more money the business generates, and the stronger it is.

Many people think that making money is hard but the fact is that *managing money is harder than making it*. Once your business is established and money starts flowing in, you will have to develop the necessary skills to manage that money. Many businesses fail not because of faulty products or an absence of paying clients; they fail because of financial mismanagement by the owners.

As the business deals with money, you will develop many financial skills. Some of the major skills are as follows:

1. Costing and pricing.

2. Budgeting.

3. Cash flow projection and management.

4. Reading and understanding financial statements such as the income or profit and loss statement, the balance sheet and the cash flow statement.

5. Presentation of business plans and financing proposals to banks and investors.

Among the financial skills you will definitely need to develop and utilize will be cash flow management. This is because cash flow is like the business's life blood. *As blood is to the human body and petrol is to a car, cash is to the business.* Your business will stand firm or waver depending on how well you are able to both generate and apply the cash it generates.

When you are an employee, you have the assurance of a fixed amount of money becoming available to you every payday. So you can make plans with a lot more certainty. Not when you are in business, unless you have a contract with a client under which your business earns a fixed amount of money or you have a lot of spare cash around you.

In business, you make a lot of money one day and the next you do not make any at all. So you have to spread what you make over the times you don't make any so that your business continues to function. Like Joseph in the Bible, you will have to store up during the times of abundance in order to survive the lean periods.

Cash flow mismanagement is the single most important reason many strong businesses fall. Cash makes businesses stay alive. The more cash the better. And the faster it flows through the business, the more growth.

When cash gets tied up for instance in physical assets such as buildings, vehicles or inventory, or creditors don't pay on time, the business will crunch to a halt. Some business owners make the mistake of concentrating on investing in physical assets such as buildings and machinery that they don't have cash to work with. Then it becomes a case of being 'asset rich but cash poor.' This situation can force the business to go into unnecessary borrowing or even receivership if the debtors establish that they can get their money back by selling your assets rather than giving you time to pay your way out.

As I have recounted in Volume 1, this is what happened to one of the companies I worked for in the early 1990s. The company owned many properties such as houses and flats, factories and office buildings throughout the country worth millions of Kina, but it did not have cash to fund its day-to-day operations. When the bank saw that it could sell off the assets and recoup its money, it scooped in with receivers who shut the company down in a day and started selling everything. By doing this they freed up the cash that was tied up in the properties, plant and equipment to get their money back.

SKILL # 5: NEGOTIATION

We have negotiated with others at one time or another. As children, we have made deals with our siblings either to our advantage or to cover up for our wrongs. As young people we have negotiated with people we are affectionate with. As employees we have negotiated contractual terms with prospective employers. So we have some crude skills with us.

In fact we all have the skills discussed in this Chapter to some extent. We were born with them. But when in business, we display these skills and develop them more because a lot is stake.

If you are like most people, when you heard the word 'negotiate,' you would have imagined fast-talking wheelers and dealers or hard-nosed penny pinchers that drive hard bargains. Yes, there are people like that who sit across negotiation tables who think of nobody else but themselves and their interests. But you do not have to be such a person to have things flowing your way. There are times to be firm, and there are times to just let the other party seem to have their way.

You learn negotiation skills more in business than in Government. In Government, it is the *public interest* at stake; in business, it is *your own survival* at stake. So you negotiate better.

If you were selling something to a client as somebody else's salesperson, you will find that when the client makes a counter-offer, you have to defer to your boss. You can stall for time. But when you are the boss, you make decisions and cut deals on the spot. When the other parties talk with you, they approach you differently than if you sent them one of your employees. They know that you can write a cheque right there and then if necessary.

One of the times you find negotiation necessary is when discussing prices. Some prices are fixed so there is little room for negotiation but you may need to discuss discounts. The prices of other goods change at every transaction. This may make price negotiation necessary at every transaction.

For instance, my background is in international coffee trading. Coffee exporters negotiate prices everyday with overseas buyers. If you are in the coffee business and are ill informed of developments in the world coffee market, overseas buyers can cut good deals for themselves at your expense. It makes knowledge of the market essential. In fact, export managers sit up all night watching the New York and London coffee exchanges as well as negotiating transactions because of time differences between Papua New Guinea and the United States and Europe. When it is night here, it is day time over there. So our exporters have to stay awake in order to talk to buyers.

The introduction of electronic mail (email) has made life very easy for people in the export/import business especially when dealing with clients in different time zones. Buyers and sellers can communicate by email, but many people still find it necessary to talk and negotiate with their clients on the telephone. It gives a more personal touch as international trade is now conducted increasingly on the basis of personal relationships.

Another important occasion where negotiation skills will come into play is when you are interviewing and recruiting members of your team. In the usual situation where the number of job seekers exceeds the number of vacancies, the people being interviewed will take whatever terms and conditions you offer. Their thinking will be that if they don't take it, somebody else will.

However, when it comes to recruiting for special skills and experience, you will find yourself negotiating because not many people possessing the set of skills and experience you are looking for are around. In such situations, you will find some interviewees negotiating hard, so your skills will come into play.

SKILL # 6: MARKETING

One of the first things you will find as a self-employed person is that in order for you to make money, you have to market yourself and your product or service. You have to get your target market to know what you are offering. In other words, you have to tell and sell.

This may involve writing introductory letters, knocking on the doors of potential buyers and making cold calls, advertising in a newspaper or other media outlet, sending an advisory note to people on your electronic mailing list, or advertising your product or service on the Internet through a website, a blog, or on social media such as Facebook and LinkedIn.

You will soon realise that having a fine product is not really as important as getting people to know about it and buy it. Your product or service can be perfect for your target audience, but if it is not known by them, it will not sell. On the other hand, you can have an inferior product but if you market it well, it can become a top seller.

Marketing is really about influencing people to believe that your product is the best there is on the market. It is about developing market perception about the unique qualities of your product, and how it can meet their needs or make their lives better. There are many relatively low quality products selling well due to the perception that they are good because the sellers invest a lot of money into marketing those products. There are also very good products which do not sell well because of poor market perception which is a reflection of poor marketing.

You might find that establishing a network of sales people is the best strategy for you. Or you might find that direct sales to customers works best.

Marketing is an area I have been grappling with since taking up book publishing as a business. Most people that have read my books have told me that the books are very inspirational and motivational, but getting the books before a large proportion of my audience is something I have yet to develop and establish as a system. I don't have a marketing system in place.

All the books I have sold so far are through *ad hoc* marketing activities such as book launches, writing letters, visiting schools, approaching booksellers, selling at seminars, setting up a personal blog on the Internet, posting on Facebook, etc. I have not promoted the books through media advertisements or established a website to sell my books to an international audience, for instance. The result is that I have not sold as many books as I could.

I know that people like the way I write and the subjects I write about. I am a *best-writing author*, but I know that when I develop marketing skills and sell thousands or hundreds of thousands of copies, I will become a *best-selling author*. I am working towards that end.

SKILL # 7: COMMUNICATION

Today's economic system operates on information. The more people know, the more competitive they are in the market place. That is why *"Be the first to know"* was the motto of a major TV channel like CNN several years back.

If you know something ahead of your competition, you have an advantage over them. And this does not mean having access to privileged information for weeks or months. It can mean as short as a few minutes, because today's information and communication technology (ICT) has enabled everyone to have access to instant or 'real-time' information.

The Internet is the most powerful medium of communication today, providing information to people as events take place. So if you know something a few minutes ahead of your competition, you can profit from that information.

Communicating effectively means investing in an appropriate scale of ICT for your business. For instance, you will definitely need to establish an email account. In today's world, letters and faxes are unfashionable. If you cannot provide an email address to clients, you are considered out of date and ancient. You might even find that you need a website to sell your products more cost-effectively. Handing out a business card with a www.abc.com address at the bottom makes you look modern and current.

I have met many business people who do not know how to send text messages. When you send them a message on their mobile phone, they will call you instead of replying through a text message. If you are one of those people, you have to make it your business to learn how to send and receive messages on your mobile phone. Texting is now part of communication in the business world. It is also cheaper than making a call on the mobile phone.

Communication also means being in touch with your clients on a constant basis. It means continuously finding out what their needs are and developing ways to meet them better. It means telling your clients what steps you are taking to improve your systems and procedures to be a better supplier or buyer as the case may be. It means providing back-up services after selling to them. It means establishing procedures for receiving comments and feedback from your clients.

Once again, a website which is constantly updated is a powerful means of communicating with everyone that has an interest in your business. You cannot afford not to have a website in today's business world.

SKILL # 8: PUBLIC SPEAKING

Surveys done in the United States have shown that the Number One fear people have is that of speaking in public. It affects people from all walks of life. I guess it is the same everywhere in the world.

It has also been found that public speaking is a skill every successful entrepreneur has identified as a major factor contributing to their success. Warren Buffet, for example, who used to be shy and timid but developed the ability to speak by taking courses and practicing constantly, has stated that in his opinion, as much as 50% of the success of any business bears some relation to the owner's ability to speak in public.

Speaking in public is a skill you will be forced to learn as a business person because a lot of your activities will involve speaking – to bankers, clients, employees, potential equity partners, legislators, members of fraternities, etc. There will come times when you will be required to make presentations before large crowds as a business leader. The ability to speak up and speak well, and articulate your ideas and plans, will have a bearing on the success of your business. It will also raise your profile as a person.

If you lack the skill, you will need to practice speaking. As it is the case for any skill, public speaking can be learned. In that regard, one of the clubs you can consider joining is Toastmasters International. This is a worldwide organisation that was established in the United States in 1924 with the recognition that people needed to learn to speak. A Toastmasters Chapter exists in Port Moresby, with clubs in various organisations.

Speaking in public has had a significant impact on my life. Many people know me as a motivational and inspirational speaker today. I have had many people tell me that they still remember speeches I gave on various occasions many years ago, in educational institutions, churches, youth congresses and public conferences. They think that I am a natural speaker.

The truth is, I was an introvert from childhood right up to the mid-1990s. I was born in 1964 so I was very shy for the first 30 years of my life. Things changed when I was forced to preach in the church. My very first sermon lasted 15 minutes. I read out my message in English to a Pidgin congregation, all the while shaking and sweating profusely, and had nothing to say for the next 45 minutes so the pastor took over and preached a completely different sermon. The experience so embarrassed me that I vowed never to preach again. But the pastor encouraged me and gave me more opportunities to preach until I gained confidence and speaking became exciting. That was in 1991.

My first time to give a speech in public was at school graduation in 2006, after the publishing of my book *Life After Graduation*. This was followed by other opportunities to speak. I also read several books on public speaking to refine my skills. One of these books was *The Art of Public Speaking* by Dale Carnegie. Another was *How To Win Friends And Influence People* by the same author. Studying these and other books gave me a lot of confidence.

One speech I gave at the launching of a friend's book before a Prime Minister resulted in the PM directing the Education Secretary to purchase thousands of copies of our books. We both made five figure sums from the orders.

Today I write and speak for a living. Unlike 25 years ago when I first started speaking, today I get more excited the bigger the audience. I don't tremble and sweat as I did then; instead, I feel buoyed on the inside to go on the stage and speak. Actually the bigger the crowd, I think better and words flow effortlessly. When I conduct seminars, I can talk for hours and days. Speaking has raised my profile, and it pays well too.

Brian Tracy, an American best-selling author, business trainer and speaker, actually calls public speaking the highest paying profession. He and others make millions every year through speaking fees and seminars.

SKILL # 9: PROBLEM-SOLVING

Business is about taking advantage of profitable opportunities. But opportunities are usually not obvious. They usually appear in the form of problems. As someone has observed: *"Opportunities are missed by most people because they come dressed up as problems.*" The way I put it is, "*Problems and opportunities are two sides of the same coin.*" Entrepreneurs profit from solving problems.

Whatever business you get into, it will always be related to a problem or need in society. In other words, the first business you get into will be because of a problem. When you are in business, you will see many other opportunities posing as problems to be solved. While the rest of society sees problems and complains about them, you as an entrepreneur will see the same problems as opportunities. That is the way business people train themselves to think. Every time they hear people complaining, they think about how to create money-making opportunities from those complaints.

That is why you will see that when someone starts a business and succeeds in it, it is not long before he is into another business. This is the reason why most business people own more than one business. When you get into business, you will develop an eye for spotting problems and converting them into opportunities.

SKILL # 10: INVESTMENT

Another major difference in the mindsets of business owners and employees is that while employees busy themselves making sales and following up on payment from customers, business owners look for more profitable business and investment opportunities. They go out looking for ways to diversify their business activities. They always weigh out opportunities and calculate in their minds the likely rates of return for different business ideas and the likely costs involved.

When you are the business owner, you will develop an eye for spotting investment opportunities. Your mind will be filled with visions of growth and expansion while your employees concentrate on maintaining the status quo. As long as money is coming in and their benefits are catered for, employees go home satisfied with their day's work. But you, as the owner, continue to look for ways to grow your business.

It is a different mindset altogether from what you are used to when you are working for someone else.

BUSINESS EXPANDS YOU

I have given you ten of the major skills you will acquire or develop when you are in business. You may think of several more. Feel free to add those to the list.

You will agree that these skills will transform you into a different person compared with if you were just an employee. A business will help or force you to expand and grow as a person. You will definitely be a different person after several years of being in business. As Donald Trump has said, it is one of the best personal development programs you can enroll yourself on.

Think of it this way: *A business is good for the money you make as well as for the person you become.* The market forces you have to contend with as a business owner and the strategies you come up with the address them will definitely stretch, expand and transform you.

Isn't that another good reason for you to think about starting a business? Please ponder and answer that before reading further.

BECOME COMPETITIVE

COMPETITION IS THE name of the game in every sphere of life. It started the moment you were conceived. Of the millions of seed that were released by your father, only one out-did the others and fertilized your mother's egg, and the result was – yes, *you*. So you have been a competitive person right from the start. And you have been a survivor up to this moment in time.

When you reflect on your childhood days, you will recall times when you out-played your siblings in terms of gaining your parents' special affection. There were some things you did which set you apart from your other brothers and sisters which attracted your parents' attention to you. You can also remember those days when you out-ran others in school sports carnivals, or you beat your class mates in tests and examinations. You have been, and are, a competitive person. Competition is in your blood.

Let me point out to you something that you probably have never realized up to now in relation to the subject of this book, and it is this: *Both the employed and the self-employed or business people compete with others, but they compete for different reasons. Employees compete for positions and benefits while business people compete for profits.*

Business people compete against each other for the hearts and minds of consumers and their money, while employees compete to impress their bosses for titles, better salaries, perks, and privileges.

EMPLOYEES COMPETE TO CLIMB CORPORATE LADDERS

Have you noticed the intense competition for positions in the workplace? Have you noticed how dirty it can get, with job applicants attempting to out-do others in convincing potential employers as to how good they are? Are you aware that sometimes people bribe those in decision-making positions to receive favoured treatment? Some people even pledge part of their starting salaries to recruiters for a specific period if they get appointed.

What is actually happening is this: *People are vying for a starting place at the foot of the 'corporate ladder.'*

Once people get a job, they find that there is another ongoing competition where employees race and even fight each other to *climb the ladder.* Once they are able to survive the jealousy, backstabbing and false reporting and they are able to climb up the ladder, the better the benefits they receive.

But it does not take long before they realise that there are only a few rungs on the ladder and that the ceiling is lower than they thought. They find out that there is a limit to the extent to which they are able to get promotions and pay rises.

OFFICE POLITICS IS INTENSE

Jostling and wrangling for positions is intense and dirty. New recruits find that people already in the system are suspicious of them and will do everything to suppress them. People who have been in the system long usually look upon new recruits as threats to their positions. So they do everything to frustrate younger co-workers. They deprive new recruits of training opportunities and prefer to attend themselves, for instance, even though they are already over-trained.

In some organizations politicians enter the picture with nepotism and political appointments. They put their cronies and cohorts in positions. The cronies come from nowhere to take jobs ahead of career people who have made their way up through sheer hard work.

Some people even invoke the powers of darkness and engage in sorcery and witchcraft to remove people from positions or to consolidate their own.

The result is that many employees become stagnant in one position for years. Promotions and pay rises come along only once every in a while until it comes to a point where the only increment is the CPI adjustment to compensate for inflation. At this point people become stale and stagnant in their hearts and minds. They lose all enthusiasm and zeal and resign themselves to doing their bit and waiting for payday.

Some people even find out very late that the ladder they had been fighting to get on and climb up has been leaning against the wrong wall. The satisfaction and good life they hoped to receive is nowhere to be seen. They had been chasing an illusion. By the time they realise it, it is too late. Time has run out on them and the competition they engaged in has drained them of their youth, strength and vitality.

THE SELF-EMPLOYED BUILD AND OWN LADDERS

You know what you would be doing when you start your own business? Here is the answer: *You would be building and owning a ladder which other people (those with employee mindsets) will be fighting each other over.* This is a powerful 'behind the scenes' insight, isn't it?

When you build and own the corporate ladder, you get a completely different view than people who are competing to climb it. You will literally see your employees jostling for your favour. You will appreciate the games they play to out-do each other for that position you own and the benefits you offer in exchange for their time, energy, knowledge, and skills. You get the empowering feeling that you are in control. And you are because you are the boss.

Climbing corporate ladders is easy; building them is hard. But it is more rewarding building and owning ladders than climbing them.

What do you suppose is the better alternative: *To compete to climb up someone else's ladder, or to build your own?* What is better: *To supervise and manage people who aspire to climb a ladder which you mind for another person, or to own a ladder and get others to climb it?*

I propose that it is better for you to own the corporate ladder than to compete for a rung on a ladder owned by somebody else. If you agree with me, you must start your own business.

EMPLOYEES COMPETE FOR 'BREAD AND BUTTER'

If you ask a salaried person what he or she does, the answer will invariably be: "*I work for bread and butter.*" Or they might say, "*I am the bread winner.*" What they mean is that they are working to earn salaries with which they will buy and put food on the table for their families and other dependents. Buying food and meeting other expenses to sustain their lives from payday to payday is foremost on their minds.

Most working class people are so short-sighted because of this 'bread and butter' mentality. Their vision of the future goes as far as the next pay day. They cannot see any further. They work, get paid, repay their debts, buy food, meet other living expenses with what is left, and go back to work again.

They do it over until it becomes habitual, second-nature, and addictive. Once they become addicted to selling themselves for salaries, they find it hard to imagine any other way of living. They leave one job for whatever reason, and they are out looking for another one. They get terminated or laid off, and they think it is the end of them. Losing their jobs is the same as their 'bread line' getting cut off.

So the next time you compete for a job, think about what you are actually doing. Look behind the pay cheque and other perks and privileges to see the lifestyle you are actually vying for. And when you compete for promotion, what are you really fighting for? I hope it is for something better and more lasting than just 'bread and butter.'

TO BE IN BUSINESS IS TO OWN BAKERIES AND BUTTER FACTORIES

You will realise that I have used so many illustrations and word pictures in both Volume 1 and this volume. In fact if you read my other books you will find that I use different mental pictures to explain things that are difficult to perceive on the face of it. That is my style. I find that people remember stories and analogies more than mere statements of principles.

Here is another of my word pictures: *Starting a business is like building a factory to bake bread and manufacture butter.*

While people with employee mentalities work for 'bread and butter,' you are actually building a bakery and a butter factory. You are not only establishing a system through which other people will derive their livelihood from. More than that, you are establishing a system through which you will be generating much more money than you will need for your survival.

Which is better: *Working for bread and butter, or owning a bakery and a butter factory?* I submit to you that the latter is better. Why? *Because when you are hungry, you can have all the bread and butter you want. You own the bakery, and owners don't go hungry.*

When you have a job, the amount of bread and butter available to you is limited to how much your salary can buy. Again, when you lose the job, you lose your 'bread line.' But when you own an operational bakery, is there a limit to how much you can eat?

You are competitive, no doubt about that. But what you compete for is another matter altogether. I challenge you to compete to build and own a corporate ladder. I challenge you to stop working for bread and butter and start thinking about building and owning a bakery and a butter factory.

You will realise that building and owning ladders is better than climbing them; and owing factories is better than working in them. And owning a 'money printing machine' is better than operating one owned by somebody else.

When you start out in business, many people will ask what you are doing. Tell them that you are building a ladder which other people will be competing to climb. Tell them you are building a bakery and a butter factory. Tell them you are building a money printing machine.

People will take you literally and probably laugh at you or even ridicule you; others may actually perceive what you are saying. They may then go off and think about how they can build ladders, bakeries, butter factories and money machines too. You being in business can inspire others to get in the game.

GET OFF THE ENTITLEMENT MENTALITY

E MPLOYERS DO NOT possess all the knowledge, skills and expertise that their organisations require to operate efficiently and profitably. So they provide all kinds of incentives to attract other people who possess the knowledge and skills they require.

As I have discussed fully in Volume 1, employers use the leverage of incentives to gain access to other peoples' time and expertise. Such incentives can include housing, vehicles, medical insurance, school fees, shares, etc, in addition to basic salaries. Employers use these conditions to multiply the amount of time and variety of skills available to them.

Employees take up positions so that they can benefit from the entitlements covered by their contracts of employment. The contracts spell out the responsibilities of both employers and employees. All employees are focused on what they can get out of their employers.

Employers expect their employees to give them undivided attention. On the other hand, because employees commit their time and expertise to their employers, they expect the employers to look after them well. They expect the employers to stick to the terms and conditions of employment too. That is to say, the employees expect the employers to pay the entitlements as agreed in their contracts of employment. It creates a culture of expectations and dependency.

EMPLOYEES BECOME ENTITLEMENT-MINDED

What employees do not realize is that as the years go by, they become more and more entitlement-minded. The longer they remain with an employer, the better they expect their entitlements to be, regardless of how productive they are. For example, every year employees expect their salaries to increase, at least by the rate of inflation. They expect to be rewarded for loyalty.

Because of such ingrained thinking, many employees become frustrated when they do not see any improvement in their terms and conditions. When they start working, there is a lot of excitement and zeal. Many people have confided that they could not sleep the night before a job interview or their first day at work. But as the weeks, months and years go by, their excitement subsides and in some cases even dissipates.

Work life becomes monotonous. It involves doing the same things over and over for months and years. There is little challenge after they have gotten the hang of things. Work becomes routine and boring. When this happens, people start thinking how exciting it would be to get a more challenging and rewarding job.

Dissatisfaction mounts even more when the entitlements remain stagnant. They may have worked their way up from the bottom, only to realize that there is no way further up once they reach a certain point. When they turn around and see how much their employer is making every year, they wonder why they are not getting any raise.

At this stage many employees either look for "greener pastures" or allow themselves to become lazy and complacent with the result that their productivity drops. There are no more incentives and entitlements to boost their morale and keep them motivated and productive.

WORKERS' UNIONS REINFORCE THE ENTITLEMENT MENTALITY

Many times employees get into groups to press employers for better pay and other conditions. That is why there are workers' unions in almost every sector or industry. The workers mobilize themselves through these unions to demand better conditions of employment which they think they are entitled to for all the effort they put into working for their employers.

They get into groups because they realize that unless they possess special skills which employers need, generally they as workers are weak when negotiating for better terms as individuals.

Union action reinforces the entitlement mentality even further. This mentality transfers the responsibility for employees' livelihoods to employers. Some union officials press for terms and conditions which are unreasonable in the sight of employers. But what employers do not realize is that union officials are making demands based on their perception that because employees fully commit their time and strength, employers should cater for employees' every need.

When employers and employees disagree, it is usually the employees who resort to taking such actions as strikes, mass withdrawal of labour, protests, picketing of employers' offices, sabotaging, court action, industrial tribunals, etc. They do this because they are the weaker party in the negotiations. Their strength lies in acting in cohort with other employees. The larger the union, the stronger it's negotiating power.

The popular saying among unionists is, *"The strength of the wolf is in the pack, and the strength of the pack is in the wolf."* Workers need their unions to press for better conditions, and unions need the support of individual members to consolidate their power vis-à-vis employers.

DOES SUPERANNUATION REALLY CATER FOR LIFE AFTER WORK?

Employees even depend on their employers for their retirement through superannuation and pensions. When they are young and energetic, they depend on their salaries, allowances and other benefits that come from exerting physical strength on their jobs. When they are old, they depend on their superannuation savings and pensions. *All their lives from graduation to retirement and old age are in the hands of other people.*

One of the entitlements which employees in Papua New Guinea are entitled to is superannuation. As the law stands, employers with twenty employees or more must become a member of a recognized superannuation scheme. The law requires that employees save at least 6% of their net fortnightly salaries in their superannuation accounts. Employers must contribute 8.4% for each of their employees. So employees are forced to save 14.4% of their gross salaries with their chosen superannuation scheme. Some employees elect to save more than 6% of their gross pay. The maximum voluntary contribution allowed by law is 15% of gross salary.

This is good. At least employees save money for life after work. However, the most important question each contributor needs to ask is this: '*Will whatever I and my employer save and returns the super fund makes from investments plus the interest that accumulates be sufficient for me to maintain my pre-retirement standard of living?*'

In other words, will they be able to continue eating the same kinds and qualities of food they are eating, wear the clothes they are wearing, and meeting the expenses they are incurring with respect to education, medication, transport, etc. while being employed?

My personal belief is that superannuation savings will be insufficient to enable most of the contributors to maintain their pre-retirement livelihoods. The reasoning is as follows.

Working people are required to retire at sixty-five years of age. They will have left school at around twenty-five, worked and saved for forty years. The average Papua New Guinean is expected to live seventy-five years, which means that the person is expected to live at least ten years in retirement and old age, perhaps more.

The question posed above can be answered by dividing the total savings at retirement by the net (or take-home) salary. Assume for instance that someone has K300,000 in his superannuation account. Assume further that K100,000 of that is from the employee's 6% contribution, while the balance of K200,000 is from the employer's 8.4% contribution plus accumulated interest over the years. The K200,000 will be taxed at 2% while his contribution of K100,000 is tax-free. Tax would be K4,000. So the total amount he will receive would be K296,000.

To find out whether this money would be sufficient to maintain his pre-retirement living standard, divide it by his current annual net salary. If we assume this to be K60,000 per annum, the super fund savings will cover the person for only five years.

Generally, the higher the pre-retirement net pay, the shorter the time span superannuation savings will cater for. If the retiree tries to spread the money over the next ten years of life after retirement, his standard of living will drop by 50%. That is very significant.

The majority of Papua New Guineans are reckless spenders. That is why the Government has instituted superannuation schemes in the first place. Most workers if given the chance will spend everything they get into their hands. So superfunds are in fact 'forced savings' for the working class.

Many workers actually borrow out their superannuation savings to meet various expenses while still being employed so their balances at retirement would be low.

COULD THE IDEA THAT SUPERANNUATION WILL LOOK AFTER YOU IN OLD AGE BE A MYTH?

This raises a pertinent question: *"Could the idea that superannuation will look after you well in old age be a myth?"*

What I have noticed about working people is that generally they do not save enough to sustain their pre-retirement lifestyles; they don't have savings of their own; and they spend most of their retirement money within the first few years of leaving work. Most workers then return to a village life much like their relatives who had never worked for a job. In most instances the relatives are better off than those who have held jobs.

Village people know how to survive on basic food, vegetables and cold water, work on the land and walk long distances on foot, while people who have held paid jobs do not. Such people have so conditioned their bodies to crave processed food such as tinned fish and rice that when they return to their villages, they age fast as they try to adjust to village food. Many in fact don't return to their villages because their relatives have taken up the family lands.

My point is this: *Don't depend on others for your livelihood, both when you are young and when you are old.* Become financially independent as early in your life as possible.

Sadly, many people develop the entitlement mindset once they start working at a job. They become too dependent on their employers for their livelihood, which is a very risky way to live life. They also believe that their superannuation savings will adequately cater for their lives after they stop working.

This may be true for some people but is not generally true for every working person. The idea that the super fund will look after you when you leave your job may be a myth which people blindly believe just because the super funds and the Government say so.

WHEN ALL IS SAID AND DONE, IT'S EVERY MAN FOR HIMSELF

When people become self-employed, they free themselves from the entitlement mentality. They become responsible for their own lives and livelihoods.

When you think about it, there is really nobody who is responsible for your life. You are responsible for your own life. This truth will become clear to you when you work for yourself. You will realize that you are responsible for putting food on the table, paying your school fees, meetings other necessary expenses.

A job introduces the idea that somebody else is responsible for your life because you are committing your time to serving that person. Such a mentality is deceptive, because in reality, everybody is concerned for themselves.

Everybody has their own personal interest at heart. People may seem to be thinking about your interests when you work for them but when you take off the covers, you will discover that it is really every man for himself.

In good times you may be the employer's best friend. But when times become tough for him, it will be either him or you. Usually, it will be you who must get the boot while he survives. It is you who may need to go without a fortnight's salary due to cash flow problems. My favourite saying is this: *"When life gets tough for the employer, the employee gets going."*

Ask every person that was laid off because their employer had financial difficulties, and they will tell you that what I am saying is true. I know this to be true because I was forced to resign the last job I held because the owner of the company I was working for claimed that the business wasn't making enough money to keep me.

Just think: Why do you think somebody gives you a job? Is it because he loves you so much and does not want you to starve? Is it because he is concerned that your kids will miss out on life's opportunities if he does not give you a source of income? I am proposing to you that *the employer gives you a job for his own good.* Notice there is a full stop after the last sentence? That is the truth.

Don't be deceived. Don't develop an entitlement mentality. Come out of it. Free your mind from this myth. The truth is this: *You are responsible for your own survival.* The employer doesn't really care about you. He is ready to kick you out when you are of little or no use to him. He may tell you not to believe what I am saying because he's got money and things to back up his word while I have only words to give you. But what I am saying will come to reality when you are shown the door by the employer.

DON'T BE BLINDED BY INCENTIVES AND ENTITLEMENTS

Don't let yourself be blinded by incentives and entitlements. The employer wants you working for him so that he can become rich on the back of your skills, knowledge, time and strength. He pays you a salary which is not sufficient for you to live your dream life. That is the truth!

Have you noticed that the employer pays you just enough to keep you alive? You know why he does that? The answer is this: *Because he wants you coming back to work for him after every payday.* If he paid you more, you would save up and start your own business. That is what the majority of employers fear. They dread the day their best employees walk off to other employers or to work for themselves.

I am aware that many working people already understand that building their lives on the entitlements provided by their employers is not good for them but leaving their jobs to work for themselves is a decision fraught with a great deal of risk and uncertainty. That is understandable. I am not here to tell people to leave their jobs. The risks are real. Not having food as a self-employed person is real. Not having school fees is real. I have experienced it.

But my intention in this Chapter is to help you become uncomfortable enough to start thinking seriously about whether the entitlements provided by employers are really yours for the long haul. My contention is that they are not.

As I related in the introductory Chapter of Volume 1, when the company I was working for went broke, the company flat which I normally referred to as 'my flat' and the company car which I called 'my car' were taken away by the receivers. It was then that I realised these entitlements really did not belong to me.

But the way I was allowed to use them conditioned me to think and claim that they were mine. I was brainwashed into asserting as mine what was somebody else's. If you are entitlement-minded, you will experience what I went through when it happens to you. You have been warned.

I hope that your mind has been opened to see beyond what your physical eyes see concerning entitlements. They are not yours. You only enjoy them so long as you hold the job. When the job goes, the entitlements go with it.

I also hope that you realize how unsafe it is to depend on your superannuation savings to sustain your life after retirement. If you care to look around, you will see that most workers are worse off after they retire. Only a few wise ones live better while the majority live in poverty and struggle after retiring from work.

Needless to say, only your own business will get you off the entitlement mentality; and only your own business will enable you to become financially independent.

STOP SURVIVIVG AND START LIVING THROUGH EARLY RETIREMENT

WHEN MOST PEOPLE hear the word "retirement," they immediately think of the time when somebody has reached a certain age which requires him or her to leave work because he or she is physically old and weak.

Every country in the world has an official retirement age. For most professions in Papua New Guinea it used to be fifty-five years but recently the Government increased it to sixty-five years.

What the law says is that you must stop working for money when you reach the retirement age but it does not stop you from retiring early. This means that you can retire earlier than the official retirement age. You can retire when you are younger if you want to. You can beat the official retirement age.

I do not mean for you to stop working and living at other peoples' expense. That is not retirement; that is plain laziness and parasitic.

What I do mean is you coming to that place where all your needs are met by your businesses and investments so you can afford to stop working for money. *Retirement really means to stop surviving and to start living.*

Unless you inherit wealth from your parents, win the lottery, or marry someone who is rich, only self-employment or business can enable you to retire when you are still young. A business is your vehicle to the land of financial and time freedom.

If you work for somebody else all your life, you will never become financially independent and free. You will develop an addiction to depending on your fortnightly pay. Most of your life will be regulated by the employer. You will work until the law forces you out of the workforce when you are least prepared financially as well as mentally and emotionally. You will find it difficult adjusting into a life of no work and no pay.

YOU CANNOT DO MUCH WHEN YOU ARE OLD

Unless you control your spending, the pay you receive will generally not be adequate for you do something for yourself like establishing and running a part-time business. So you will work until you reach retirement age.

You will be so busy going to work, getting paid, paying your bills, and going back to work, until you become old. You will not realize that time is running out on you until it is too late. Ask yourself: *How much can you do for yourself at sixty-five or even fifty-five years of age?* Not much, I would say.

In Papua New Guinea, sixty-five years is really several years away from old age, if you live that long. Even if you want to do something for yourself with your retirement lump sum or superannuation savings, it will be too late to make up for lost time.

You might not have the physical strength and stamina to go into business. The world might be too competitive for you. You might even be afraid to do anything at all for fear of losing all your life's savings, so much so that you spend everything and end up broke.

THE FOUR QUARTERS OF LIFE AFTER SCHOOL

Life can be divided into three main periods. The first twenty-four years are made up of childhood and education. They can be labeled the 'learning years.' This is followed by the next forty years commencing at age twenty-five and ending at sixty-five. They can be labeled the 'earning years.'

The remaining years of retirement and old age can be labeled the 'yearning years.' This is the time when people sit down and think about all the opportunities they missed and wish that they could rewind the clock so that they could make up for them. Their dominant wish is, *"If only I was young again."*

Here is how the years look:

1 – 24	Childhood and School	Learning
25 – 65	Working for Money	Earning
66 +	Retirement and Old Age	Yearning

Life during the Earning Years can be divided into four quarters as follows:

Quarter # 1	25 – 35 years
Quarter # 2	35 – 45 years
Quarter # 3	45 – 55 years
Quarter # 4	55 – 65 years

It is akin to a football game. The game here involves playing with money, not a ball. It is the game of money in the arena or stadium of the economy.

That is how society has been ordered. Most people do not realize that they are falling into a plan that was set in place by people who designed the economic system. The system has been designed to make a few people rich on the back of the physical strength, knowledge and skills of the majority. Because of ignorance, people go to school, get jobs, pay bills and go back to work until they are physically weak.

I propose to you that you need to take a different route. Don't follow the beaten path. Think different, and be different. Don't submit to the system. Break away from its clutches. Let the ignorant live the pre-arranged lifestyle. You know better (or if you didn't, now you do).

My proposition to you is that you deserve to enjoy freedom and life when you are young. The system is geared towards a lifestyle of bondage and servitude. Life is too short to just lie down and accept what you are offered. You need to stop depending on an employer's pay cheque.

You need to stop working for money at some stage while you are still young. You need to stop working and start living.

Only in self-employment can you find the possibility for that kind of freedom.

If you put together what I have said in this Chapter with the preceding one, you will realise that the mentality that superannuation will cater for your life in retirement is hazardous. It is better that you take personal responsibility for your retirement and plan to retire when you are still young and strong than when you are old and feeble from years of minding other peoples' businesses.

IT'S WHEN YOU DON'T NEED
MONEY THAT YOU CAN SERVE

People go to work because they need money. For most workers, money is the only motivation for them getting up every working day. The pay cheque is the magnet that attracts them. At the bottom of their hearts they hate the jobs. But they need to work because if they don't, they won't eat.

When I say that a business can enable you to retire early, I don't mean that you must resign from your job. You can if you want to, but you don't have to. You can still go to work but when you have a business that makes money for you, money will not be the sole reason for you going to work. You go to work because you *want* to, not because you *need* to. You go to work for reasons other than the pay cheque.

For instance, you don't need money but you still go to work because you like the atmosphere in the office, or the job provides you the opportunity to meet different people, or you realize that the job enables you to make a contribution to society with your set of skills, knowledge, and expertise.

In other words, it is the job that gives you the satisfaction, not money. You don't care if the employer cuts your pay or doesn't acknowledge your contribution. He stops paying you and you still go to work. Why? Because you don't need the money; you love your job and the contribution it enables you to make to the employer or society at large that you are willing to work for free.

Is this impossible? You wouldn't think so, but there are people in the world who actually work for free. Why would they do such a thing? The answer is because they have so much money from their businesses and investments that they find fulfillment in their lives by volunteering their services for free.

It is when you reach such a point that you come to appreciate what service means. It is only when you are financially free that you truly serve others. As long as you work for money, you cannot serve people. When you don't need money is the moment you really serve others.

Isn't this something you can aspire to experiencing in your life? Do you truly want to be of service to your community or country? If the answer welling up on the inside of you is 'Yes,' I encourage you to start your business soon.

A business is a powerful vehicle that can carry you from your current financial situation and state in life to the place where you are financially free. Then you can retire from working for money, and if you still want to work, you do so because you want to be a blessing to your employer, the community and the world.

WHO WILL WORK IF EVERYBODY IS IN BUSINESS?

This is a question I get asked regularly in my seminars. My response is that the fact is, not everybody will get into business. Why? Because the conditioning by the education and economic systems is such that people fear taking risks. They would rather exist in the safe zone of paid jobs than venture out to start businesses.

Once peoples' minds are programmed to look for jobs, they will not even think about starting their own businesses. Just look at graduates of business schools. Most of them graduate with certificates, diplomas, degrees and even MBAs and immediately look for jobs! Not many think about starting their own businesses immediately after graduating!

My message to people who ask this question is, *"Don't worry about others; you start your business. There will never be a shortage of workers."*

My secondary reply is that even though it will never happen, it would be good if everyone was in business! Why? Because it would turn the job market from a buyers' market to a sellers' market, meaning there would be too many jobs and not enough jobseekers.

This would force employers to improve their terms and conditions of employment in order to attract workers. In this way wealth would be more equitably distributed and there would be less poverty among the working people. The gap between the rich and poor would be smaller, and the contention between classes would subside. Society would be more prosperous and safer.

As it is, the sheer number of job-seekers gives too much economic power to the rich, all of whom are business owners.

My third response is that people get the wrong idea about business. They think about resigning from jobs to get into business full-time. This is not necessarily so. People can own businesses while keeping their jobs. In todays' world, millions of people have side businesses. The internet has provided the greatest opportunity for side hustles.

Many people actually make millions from those businesses without having any employees. Such businesses are fully automated which means that they sell digital products such as e-books, online courses, audios, videos, photographs, etc. through websites which have shopping carts and payment gateways. Purchases are made using credit cards and other payment systems such as PayPal so once the business system are set up, the proprietors do not exert any effort at all apart from checking their bank balance.

Whether you get into business full-time or part-time isn't the issue; the issue is that you get into it. Again, the sooner you do the better.

PROVIDE BETTER EDUCATION FOR YOUR CHILDREN

M OST PARENTS WOULD like to see their children getting the best education possible. Notice I am saying *most* and not *all*, because some parents do not seem to care whether their children go to school at all, and where. This is indicated by the way they spend their money. They throw their money around and when it comes to school fee time they do not have any money. Thousands of young children do not go to school because of careless parents who mismanage their money.

Many such parents run desperately to the banks or money lenders to borrow money to pay school fees. It is as if the parents just remembered that they have kids to send to school!

How irresponsible! Countless children have been forced out of school because of school fee problems, not because their parents cannot afford the fees but because they have mismanaged the money they earned from various sources. Children pay hefty penalties for their parents' foolishness.

SCHOOL FEES ARE VERY HIGH

Education was almost free in Papua New Guinea just after independence in 1975. Parents did pay something but not as much as they do today. I remember that community school fees were K5 in the late 1970s and high school fees were less than K75 for day students and K150 for boarding.

When we were at University during the late 1980s, the Government not only paid our fees; we were paid allowances as well! The National Scholarship (or Natschol) allowance was K13 per fortnight at the time I exited university in 1988. On top of that, they paid us book allowances. Even our travel costs were met fully by the Government.

During the 1990s the Government introduced the "user-pay" policy. Under this policy, people who benefited from most services were required to pay for them wholly or in part. School fees were raised substantially and student allowances received by tertiary students were abolished.

Today, fees range from K100 at elementary school to in excess of K15,000 per year at university. In addition to that, parents have to meet all other costs associated with their kids' education.

The result is that education has become very expensive in the country. Thousands of students stay out of school every year because the parents cannot afford to pay the fees. With the way things are going, it will not be long before only the children of the well-to-do go to school while the children of the poor stay at home.

The result is that the gap between the rich and the poor or the "haves" and the "have-nots" will widen further. One consequence of this, which bears repeating, will be that while the "haves" control the offices and the corridors of power, the "have-nots" will control the streets, so much so that the "haves" will feel increasingly fearful of enjoying what they have in full view of the "have-nots."

Unfortunately, an increasing number of those children who do not go to school due to school fee problems belong to working people. Most working people have three or more children going to school at the same time. Because parents have not spaced their children, they find that several children have to go to school one or two grades apart from each other.

The parents can manage while these kids are in primary school, but the moment they enter secondary school, they immediately run into problems. And when the children go to tertiary institutions, most parents find that some children have to sacrifice for others. The pay they receive from their jobs is just not sufficient when living costs are taken into account. Unfortunately, it is usually the girls who sacrifice so that their brothers can continue in school.

At time of writing the Government is providing free education under its Tuition-Fee Free Policy but there is no guarantee that this will continue perpetually. Changes in regime or hard economic times can force a change of policy. Even with this policy, the ultimate responsibility for children's education is in the hands of parents.

HIGH COSTS OF LIVING

Costs of living have risen substantially in the country, particularly after the local currency was devalued in September

1994. Prior to that the value of the Kina was maintained at U$S1.20. Imagine that! I used to travel a lot to Europe and Asia during the early 1990s and I used to marvel at the fact that the Kina could actually buy more US dollars.

Following the devaluation the Kina was allowed to float freely against other currencies. Immediately the local currency depreciated against all the major currencies, in particular the US dollar, the Australian dollar and the British pound. The effect was that prices of imported goods rose quickly. To buy goods from overseas suppliers, importers in the country needed more Kina to buy the same basket of goods. With Papua New Guinea being an import-dependent country, living costs skyrocketed. And they have not come down since.

Rising costs of living and the "user pay" policy have combined to keep the majority of working people struggling to make ends meet. After income tax and rent, school fees are the largest single cost faced by working class Papua New Guineans. The sad fact is that whether children go to school and what schools they attend is dictated by the pay their parents receive.

EDUCATION STANDARDS HAVE DROPPED SUBSTIANTIALLY

I believe that the public education system's standards have fallen drastically compared to the 1970s and 1980s. We have had several reforms to the system but standards have not risen as expected. On the contrary, they have taken our children backwards.

One of the major changes under the Outcome-Based Education curriculum was the introduction of Elementary Schools taught by Grade Ten and Twelve leavers, in Pidgin and local vernaculars! The ages seven to ten are very crucial formative years, yet children are not being adequately equipped for later stages of their school lives. They are supposed to live and compete in an ever-changing global economy, yet they are not being adequately prepared during their foundational years.

I receive emails from students from many parts of the country. I can testify that their written English is very poor. I have also heard from university lecturers that the language used by most of their students is poor.

I attend many student meetings in which students speak more in Pidgin than in English. They cannot communicate confidently in English. And they cannot speak for any length of time without changing between English and Pidgin. I should say they start in English and end in Pidgin. Read through posts on Facebook and you will know what I mean.

Recently the University of Goroka – the premier teacher training institution in the country – reported that over 60% of first-years failed a basic language skills entry test. This makes me wonder where the reforms have taken the country to, seeing that English is the main language of international trade and commerce. The fact that our trainee teachers cannot speak well in English is frightening because they are the ones who will stand before our children in the classrooms and teach in broken English.

The reforms were introduced in recognition of the fact that the majority of young people will return to their villages after school. So they have to learn in the languages they will use. But we live in a global village where communication in English is essential. The reforms have made our young people fit into the local society but not the modern world.

Another observation I have made is that most of what our children learn is irrelevant or at least inappropriate to live in the 21ˢᵗ Century. It is not surprising then that our political, bureaucratic, and business leaders send their kids to private and international schools. They do not have much faith in our own system.

To make matters even worse, many of teachers have lost all sense of professionalism and commitment. Most have lost confidence in the leadership and morale is very low due to unfavourable working conditions such as low pay and lack of accommodation. Many teachers roam in town or play cards and poker machines when they should be in their classrooms teaching. Their dressing is very poor too. If you met some of them on the streets, you would not tell that they are teachers.

This drop in the standard of public education system is a worldwide phenomenon. In many developed countries many private education institutions have sprung up. The standards of these private schools are much higher than the public schools.

Another development is that of home schooling. In many parts of the world the formative years of school are being conducted at home rather than in traditional schools. And now with the internet, many children are getting educated in the comfort of their homes under the supervision of their parents.

I have said the above to make this point: *I am convinced that the only way the children of working class people can receive good education is when the parents can afford to send them to better schools.* And the only way that can happen is for the parents to go into business, whether it is part-time or full-time, because employers are not going to raise salaries to enable parents to give their children the highest quality of education. Unless people go into business, even as full-time farmers, their children will not receive good education.

BUSINESS IS THE ONLY WAY YOUR KIDS CAN RECEIVE GOOD EDUCATION

What I am saying is this: If you are a working person, you need to realize that where your children go to receive their education is limited by how much you earn and how much you can afford; and how much you earn is under the control of your employer. So indirectly, the employer determines which school your children attend.

If you work for a company, check where your bosses' children are receiving their education. You will generally find that it is not in the same place your kids are getting theirs. Why is this? It is because they have businesses which pay for their children to go to better schools. You work hard for them from eight to five each day to enable them to pay their school fees. They pay you a salary which is not enough for you to send your children to the same schools their children attend.

If you want to send your children to schools of your choice, you can do two things: You can lower your living costs and save every year so that you can afford the high fees charged by private schools, or you can increase your income; you can live *below* your means, or you can *increase* your means.

To reduce living costs to cater for the high fees charged by good schools is really out of the question unless you are a highly-paid executive. So in order to send your children to really good schools, I am saying that you need to raise your income, and the only way you can do that is to go into business.

If you dream of your children attending overseas schools, again you need to go into business for yourself. If for no other reason, then just for your children you need to consider going into business. The more money you have, the better schools your children can attend. You cannot have the kind of money you need to do that by working for somebody else. Only your own business will empower you to give your children a better education.

SCHOOL FEES ARE DEDUCTIBLE EXPENSES FOR BUSINESS OWNERS

I stated in Chapter 18 of Volume 1 that there are many tax advantages available to business owners which employees are not entitled to. One of those is the cost associated with educating children.

If you own a business and you have an employment contract with your own company, you can write the contract to state that the company will meet your education expenses. Then you can legitimately charge those costs against the company as employee-related expenses. The Tax Office will accept those costs as 'deductible expenses,' which have the effect of raising the company's expenses, lowering its profits, and hence its taxable income.

The good thing about owning a business is that the business owner passes the cost onto the business. In reality, the fees are paid by the business's clients. A business is a vehicle through which products or services are supplied to the public. In the process of buying the business's products or services, the customers end up paying the owner's school fees. Seen in that way, a business is a vehicle used by business owners to transfer their costs including school fees to other people to ensure that their children receive the best education.

In conclusion, if you would like your children to receive the best education, you must start our own business.

BEAT AND RIDE
ON INFLATION

INFLATION REFERS TO a general increase in the price of goods and services over a period of time. It is measured as a percentage increase from a previous level. The three main variations to inflation are:

- *Hyperinflation.* This is unusually rapid inflation. In extreme cases, this can lead to the breakdown of a nation's monetary system. One of the most notable examples of hyperinflation occurred in Germany in 1923 when prices rose 2,500% in one month, and recently in the African country of Zimbabwe.

    A popular story in the German experience goes that one housewife took a wheelbarrow full of cash to the bakery to buy a loaf of bread. While she was inside the bakery, someone emptied the cash on the street and took the wheelbarrow away. The wheelbarrow had more value to the thief than the money.

    In all countries that have experienced hyperinflation, basic goods and services have been priced in the hundreds of thousands and even millions of the local currency. Prices have been known to change every day as well. In the Zimbabwean case, an egg is said to have cost more than one billion Zimbabwe dollars!

- *Stagflation.* This is the combination of high unemployment and economic stagnation with inflation. This happened in industrialized countries during the 1970s when a bad world economy was combined with the Organisation of Petroleum Exporting Countries (OPEC) raising crude oil prices. Economies went into recession while prices rose at the same time, causing so much hardship for millions of people.

- *Deflation* happens when there is a fall in the general price level. This is the opposite of inflation, and is what Japan has been facing in recent times. Deflation is in fact what Governments fear more than inflation. That is why most of the major countries in the developed world have reduced their interest rates to as low as zero in order to resuscitate their economies following the aftermath of the Global Financial Crisis which started around 2008.

  The main instrument used was a policy called Quantitative Easing under which Central Banks reduced interest rates and printed money. It was aimed at causing or generating inflation in their economies to combat deflation.

Contrary to what most citizens think, Governments actually *desire inflation* and *hate deflation*. The monetary policy goal of Central Banks is *price stability*, not price reduction. Generally, Governments love steadily rising prices and fear falling prices.

This is because high and rising prices attract investors into their countries. When prices are low and subdued, consumers are happy but investors and business people aren't. So, Governments are happy as long as there are steady rises in prices. They actually work to induce inflation in the economy. It is when prices rise too much that Governments are very careful because then the people will notice and vote them out of office.

Inflation is usually referred to as a "hidden tax." This is because even as income tax reduces the consumer's take-home pay, inflation reduces the consumer's purchasing power. One (income tax) is more apparent than the other (inflation), but the effect on income and living standards is the same. When tax and inflation combine, which is to say they rise together, the negative impact on consumers' standards of living is multiplied.

HOW INFLATION IS MEASURED

Inflation is usually measured by the Consumer Price Index or CPI, based on a 'basket of goods.' The 'basket' represents the most common items people in the country spend their money on. In Papua New Guinea, the National Statistical Office (NSO) is responsible for collecting information on the prices of the goods and services on a monthly basis in order to determine the rate of inflation.

The 'basket' and formula was established in 1977 and has not changed much since. This has raised a lot of concerns recently with many commentators pointing out that the range of items people purchase has changed over the years, yet the NSO uses a 'basket' that is over 30 years old. What people therefore suspect is that the inflation rate the NSO publishes is most probably under-estimated and gives a false impression of the increase in prices consumers are faced with.

EFFECTS OF INFLATION

Inflation affects different people in different ways. For the purposes of this book, I would like to discuss how inflation affects salaried people compared with people who run their own businesses.

Salaried people work for fortnightly incomes. What they receive is fixed over a year, and sometimes for three or more years. With a given income they buy a certain basket of goods and services to establish and maintain their living standards. Depending on their incomes and lifestyles, some people receive enough to save consistently while others find that they cannot save at all. Most working people have high living standards compared to the unemployed or those in the villages, which means that their costs of living are high.

Generally, the higher the income, the higher the standard of living as well as the costs associated. The more people earn, the more they spend.

When the prices of goods and services increase, working people find that they cannot buy the same quantities or basket of goods as they could do previously. The quantities of consumer items remain the same but it takes more money to purchase them. To maintain quantity, people need to fork out more cash. Many times they trade quality for quantity, meaning that they go for lower quality goods.

A simple example would be of a one kilogram packet of Trukai rice which costs K6.00. If inflation in a year is 5%, the same packet of rice will cost K6.30 the following year. Notice that the quantity of rice hasn't changed. It remains at one kilogram. One kilogram will always be one kilogram. What changes is the amount of money involved.

What can be said therefore is that inflation takes place when the value of money falls against goods and services. The impression on the surface is that prices have risen but the truth is that money had depreciated against good and services. When a currency depreciates, its value declines against other currencies; likewise, when there is inflation, a currency's value declines against goods and services.

Returning to the example, a housewife would need 30 toea more for every kilogram of rice she purchases for her household. If it is a ten kilogram bag, the housewife would need K3 more. If we assume that she buys rice for a family who needs ten kilogram bag a fortnight, the family would need K78 more every year [K3 x 26 fortnights] to buy the same bag of rice.

If the family is large (which is not unusual in the Papua New Guinea setting), one ten kilogram bag might not be sufficient for a fortnight. They might actually need a 25 kilogram bag, considering not only the immediate family but also members of the extended family. In this case, the breadwinner will need to increase his budget for rice alone by K7.50 per fortnight or K195 in a year. Note that this is on account of a 5% or 30 toea increase in the price of Trukai rice.

Imagine that the same calculation is done for all the common items a typical working class family buys. When added together, you can imagine the family needing so much more to maintain the basket of goods they were buying the previous year.

The family can go on increasing its expenses on food and other items as long as their income keeps pace with inflation. In reality, income rarely increases with inflation. Any CPI adjustment employers make to salaries normally comes at least one year later, and usually the adjustment does not cover the full extent of the rise in prices. Employers are also faced with rising costs of operations so they are usually reluctant to compensate their employees the full extent of inflation.

What this means is that people working for salaries suffer when the prices of basic goods and services rise. The 'purchasing power' of their income falls every time prices rise without a proportionate increase in their income. This usually leads to a drop in living standards.

The other thing about inflation is that the CPI records the average rise in prices of the goods in the 'basket.' What it does not show is the actual rise in the price of the individual items in the basket. The Government might announce that the average prices of goods in the 'basket' have risen by 5% but in actual fact the prices for an individual item such as a loaf of bread may have risen by 15% and tinned fish by 20%. It is also possible that the prices of some of the goods in the basket have fallen.

NOMINAL VERSUS REAL INCOMES

Economists usually make a distinction between *nominal* and *real* income. Nominal income is the actual cash which people receive, whereas real income is the cash income divided by the average price level in the economy.

An example will clarify the difference between the two types of income. Say someone is paid a gross salary of K20,000 per year. That would be his nominal income. If prices rise by 10% during the year, the employee's real income would be K18,000 [i.e. K20,000 minus 10% = K2,000].

The employee's income would lose 10% of its 'purchasing power.' The effect would be the same as the employee taking a K2,000 pay cut or suffering a rise in income tax by that amount.

If the employee's salary rises by 10% to compensate for inflation, the nominal income would be K22,000 per year but real income would be K20,000. It means the employee would buy the same quantity of goods and services he had bought with K20,000 when prices were 10% lower. The K22,000 cash is actually worth K20,000 in goods and services.

What if inflation is 10% and the employee's salary increases by only 5%? In other words, what if the employer compensates the employee only 50% of the rise in cost of living? The answer is that the employee's nominal salary would *increase* to K21,000 per year but his real income would *decline* by 5% to K19,000. He would be worse off by K1,000 compared with previous year. It would effectively be like taking one step forward and two steps back financially.

Not understanding the difference between nominal and real income is one of the major reasons why working people struggle financially. People normally look at the cash amounts more than the 'buying power' or 'strength' of those amounts. So when employees receive pay rises or CPI adjustments, they normally think that they have more money so they go out and spend more or even go into debt with the false belief that they now have more cash to service the debts.

THE TIME VALUE OF MONEY

What most people do not know is that there is a law in finance called the 'time value of money.' This law states that the real value of a given amount of money declines the further we go into the future. This is because prices usually rise every year, so a given amount can buy less and less of a certain commodity or service.

An important implication of the law is that if money is worth less in the future, it is better to have it now. In short, the time value of money says that a Kina today is better than a Kina tomorrow, next week, next month and next year.

What this law really means for employed people is that the actual value of their contractual terms and conditions, particularly their salaries over a given contract period, are not what they seem to be. The real value of total benefits is actually lower not only by the legal deductions such as tax and super fund contributions but by the 'hidden tax' of inflation.

Let me use an example to illustrate the impact of this law on salaries. Assume that someone signs a three-year employment contract whose base salary plus fringe benefits is K100,000 per year. The total contract over the period is K300,000. Let us assume that the average rate of inflation is 5% over the period. The real value of the contract has to be discounted by 5% in order to determine the real value. The picture would look like is:

Year 1		K100,000
Year 2	K100,000 less 5%	K 95,000
Year 3	K95,000 less 5%	K 90,250
Total Real Value		K285,250

The real value of the contract is K285,250, not K300,000 as it appears to be. This is of course in gross terms. The actual amount that gets credited into the employee's account every pay day is lower by the amount of income tax and other deductions.

Because most job-seekers do not understand finance, they usually grab job opportunities without thinking about what they are committing themselves to. For one thing, jobs are scarce and there is so much competition that when people are offered jobs, they don't negotiate on terms. Employers also dangle the gross figures before job applicants, making what they are offering appear to be more than it really is. They rarely explain to prospective employees what the effect of income and fringe benefits tax will be on their pay.

To explain the impact of the 'time value of money' principle is usually beyond the understanding of even the Human Resource Managers who interview employees. It is only later that the employees realize how much less they actually receive, and the fact that raging prices set them back economically.

The combined effects of income tax and inflation are such that they push employees downwards without those affected realizing what is happening. The life-story of every employee is essentially like trying to wade upstream against a strong current. Usually employees expend strength and energy fighting the financial forces of taxes, inflation and debt that are arrayed against them more than enjoying life. They get beaten by these forces.

In fact, I liken the lives of working class people to be similar to meat in a sandwich. Imagine a sandwich which is basically two pieces of bread with vegetables and meat in the middle. The top piece of bread represents low incomes and high income tax which bear downward pressure. The bottom piece represents inflation and consumption tax which exert upward pressure.

That is how the lives of working class people get squeezed like meat in a sandwich. The pressure is greater when consumer debt is added to the equation.

RIDING ON AND BEATING INFLATION

Inflation affects salaried people because their salaries are fixed for several years. So they are stuck. There is not much they can do apart from staging a protest for higher salaries. The usual consequence is reduced living standards on account of inflation. They get knocked back by escalating prices because they sell their time by the hour.

The story is different for people who sell products and services through businesses. Such people usually beat inflation because they can increase the prices of their products by more than the general rise in prices in the economy. They pass on increased costs to consumers, most of whom are working class people. In other words, business people ride on the back of inflation while their employees get trampled by it.

Let us take the example of someone who is in the business of renting out residential properties. Tenancy agreements usually stipulate that rental amounts will be adjusted for inflation. So every time prices rise, the landlord increases the rental by the published CPI percentage. The tenant therefore pays more.

If the landlord has taken a loan to buy the property, he only pays the bank the agreed amount every month so any increase in rental income resulting from inflation becomes extra cash for him. It also raises the value of his property purely because it now earns more as well as the fact that it costs much to build new houses.

At the same time, the landlord's equity on the property rises, which enables him to become wealthier every time there is a rise in the general price level. He rides on inflation to fortify his financial position. The tenant on the other hand faces the prospect of paying more to the landlord. If he is an employee who pays from his own salary, he is put back financially while the landlord rides his way to the bank.

Business people also have a better chance of realizing returns on investment that are higher than the inflation rate. By passing on increased costs to consumers, they protect and even raise their profits margins. For example, if a business aims for a gross margin of 20% and prices rise by 10%, it can increase its prices by 10% across the board so that it still realizes the 20% margin.

But if the business does well, it can exceed its target of 20%. It may realize a profit margin of 50% or even a 100% or 200% in the year, and thereby exceed inflation by many times. Obviously such a prospect is beyond someone who works for a salary.

Let me add the qualification here that there is a limit to how much business people can raise their prices on account of inflation. They are usually mindful of competition as well. If they raise their prices too much, more efficient operators will beat them in the marketplace. So sometimes business people allow their own margins to erode rather than raise prices and protect margins.

The point I am making is that business people do have the ability to adjust their prices upwards when the general prices of goods and service increase, which is something employees cannot do to their salaries. Business people can also beat inflation by the fact that if their businesses are profitable, the returns they realize are unlimited, whereas the salaries of employees are limited.

With the certainty of prices rising every year, your best bet for maintaining and improving your livelihood is starting your own business.

If you bite the bullet and take the risk of starting a business today, you have the chance to live a better life tomorrow. But if you wallow around the comforts of a paid job, you may find your living standard eroding substantially as your income remains stagnant while prices of the goods and services you buy with your after-tax income shoot through the roof.

OWN A PRIVATE PIPELINE INTO THE ECONOMY

A PIPELINE IS SOMETHING most Papua New Guineans would be familiar with. We have heard a lot about the oil pipeline that runs from the oilfields of the Hela Province to the refinery on the coast. For the past few years we have heard a lot about the liquefied natural gas (LNG) pipeline. This pipeline carries LNG from the same province to the conditioning plant outside Port Moresby for export to markets in Asia and other parts of the world.

This is good for the country, but my question is, *"Can you build your own pipeline too?"* You see, the oil and gas pipelines are parts of a bigger pipeline which exists but which we cannot see with our eyes. *What I am referring to is the pipeline of the economy.* It is the pipeline of money, not oil or gas.

The good thing about this pipeline is that it is not limited to the oil and gas fields. Rather, this pipeline of the economy crisscrosses the country, carrying money everywhere it goes. All you have to do to benefit personally from what this big pipeline carries is to build your own pipe and connect it to the main one.

A BUSINESS IS YOUR PIPELINE INTO THE ECONOMY

A paid job is an example of a pipeline through which a fixed amount of money flows to the owner (the job holder) every fortnight or month. If you hold a job, think of it as a pipeline through which you are connected to the economy. You get a share of what flows through it. However, as I have been emphasizing throughout the book, this pipeline is small, unsafe, and unsecure. You receive way below what you are capable of, and you can get disconnected anytime.

A business is a better and bigger pipeline. What the pipeline owner receives through it cannot be limited. Sometimes the pipeline doesn't carry any money to the owner; but when it does deliver, the sky is the limit as to how much the owner receives. The bigger the pipeline and the lesser the blockages in the system, the more money it carries to the owner. Unlike a jobholder who has to work himself, a business person gets other people to ensure that his pipeline fulfills its purpose.

THE PARABLE OF THE PIPELINE

The idea of a business being a pipeline is contained in a short animated video titled *The Parable of The Pipeline* which I show to participants in my *Seven Steps To Financial Freedom* seminar. It talks about two friends called Pablo and Bruno, and the different strategies they used to address their community's water problem.

The story goes that Pablo and Bruno started solving the problem by carting water from a mountain spring across the mountainside to the village using buckets. They got paid by the bucketful of water they delivered. The more trips they made back and forth in a day, the more they received.

One day Pablo got tired of carrying water so he discussed an idea with his friend Bruno. His idea was to build a pipeline into the village. But Bruno was happy with the way things were going. He saw that he was able to buy a big house and a cow and fulfill some of his other dreams with the income he was getting from carting water using his physical strength.

So Pablo decided to go it alone and use his free time to design and build a pipeline. He still carted water with buckets but used his free time to work on the pipeline. Many of his friends laughed at him. They couldn't understand why he was wasting his time and strength on this project. They thought his friend Bruno was smarter to get paid by the bucket, go to the pub often to enjoy some of his hard-earned money with his friends, and live a seemingly good life.

However, in the course of time, Bruno grew weak physically from months and years of ferrying water using his physical strength, until he came to a point where he just couldn't continue anymore. On the other hand, Pablo continued building until one day he was able to switch the water on. At this point he got paid by the litre.

His system was such that money was going into his account on a 24/7/365 basis even while he slept. Pablo could live the life of his dreams because now he had a system in place which made money for him without him doing anything physically.

The parable brings out different strategies used by people to solve the money problem in their lives. The majority of people think that getting a paid job is the way to make a living. People are indoctrinated to such an extent that when they cannot get jobs after graduating from school, they feel hopeless. Society also makes them feel that they are good-for-nothing just because they are unemployed.

Many young people in this category are filling the streets of the cities and towns of this country. Educated okay but very frustrated and angry because they cannot get the jobs they had been conditioned to expect.

Some people are like Bruno. They are lucky to get jobs and work for money using their own strength, time, and skills. They trade their time and strength, get paid, pay bills, and go back to work again. When they stop working the money stops coming in, so they have to go back to work again after each payday. Eventually they become worn out.

A minority of people are like Pablo. They choose to think differently from the crowd. They see that working for money will eventually wear them out both physically and emotionally. So they start thinking about other ways of making money. They use their minds to come up with creative ways of solving the problems of society. They establish businesses or money-making systems based on those ideas.

The more effectively and efficiently their businesses solve other peoples' problems, the better they are at meeting their own need for money. Many such people do not do anything to ensure that money flows in to enable them to live the life of their dreams because other people and systems work for them.

WHILE SOME PEOPLE ARE BUSY WORKING FOR SALARIES, OTHERS ARE BUSY BUILDING PIPELINES

Following the signing of the document containing the LNG developer's final investment decision in New York, a lot of building projects sprang up all over the country in Port Moresby, Lae, Kokopo, and Mount Hagen as well as other centres. These projects are examples of people building their own pipelines. They knew that a lot of money was going to flow in the economy so they either established or expanded existing businesses to position themselves so that they could capture as much of the money that flows in the big pipeline.

This is what other people have been doing. The question is, *"How about you?"* Isn't it time you built your own private pipeline into the economy? Isn't it time you positioned yourself to benefit in a big way from the wealth of the nation?

I propose to you that it is high time! Yes, there are high-paying jobs on offer from the developers of the LNG project and others that are associated with them. There are also jobs on offer from developers of the country's gold, copper, and oil resources. And yes, a job is a pipeline. But a business is a better and bigger pipeline which you can build, own, and operate, and benefit fully from.

A BUSINESS MAKES YOU A PIPELINE OWNER, NOT A MERE LANDOWNER!

Our friends from Hela Province and those living along the LNG pipeline route as well as those surrounding the plant site on the outskirts of Port Moresby are set to benefit as landowners. The main benefits they will receive are royalties, while the developers own and operate the pipeline. Let that be so. You need to think about becoming a pipeline owner, not merely a landowner collecting royalties. You need to actively participate in the economy, not be a passive spectator waiting for handouts. Only a business gives you the opportunity to benefit in a big way.

The beauty of being in Papua New Guinea at this point in time is that you can be based anywhere in the country and still benefit from the export of LNG and other commodities because the pipeline of the economy runs everywhere. As the economy rises like a wave, you will ride it through your business in the same way a surfer does a natural wave. As the saying goes, *"A rising tide lifts up all boats."* Yours may be a small business but it will still be lifted by a buoyant economy.

WATCH...WAIT...WISH...OR TAKE ACTION

I have met so many people who have told me that they can see opportunities for business but the time is not right. One typical excuse I have heard is, *"My children are still in school, so I cannot take any risks."* Another is, *"I don't have the experience."* A common excuse is, *"I don't have money to start a business."* These are all genuine reasons so I don't intend to argue.

What I do want to do is to report that I have met a lot of regretful people as well. They saw the opportunities but decided that they would wait for their right time. They have watched while others took action – and succeeded. Those who have been watching have kicked themselves thinking,

"*I wish I took action when the opportunity came by me.*" They watched and waited, and now all they can do is to wish in regret.

Will you be one of those people? Would you watch, wait and wish, or would you take action? You decide.

It is said that there are three types of people:

1. Those that make things happen;

2. Those that watch things happen; and

3. Those that ask "*What happened?*"

Which one of these people are you? You live in a world where opportunities abound right around you. Are you going to take advantage of them or are you going to shrink back and watch others doing it? Or are you going to deliberately blind yourself now, open your eyes later and ask, "*What happened?*"

I read somewhere that poverty is an insolent intruder whereas wealth is gentle and expects to be attracted. Poverty gatecrashes into peoples' lives while wealth waits to be invited. Watching and waiting may lead to wishing, whereas taking action now might help to push back poverty and attract wealth and abundance. It all depends on what you choose to do.

I have stated at the beginning of the book that the economic system is engineered towards making a few people rich and the rest of us poor. If you look at the background of the rich, you will find that most of them are self-made. In other words, they didn't inherit the wealth; rather they built up their wealth from scratch.

This means that even though the system is designed to keep the majority in poverty, some people have been able to beat it. And if you look closely at these people, you will definitely find that they are people who took massive action to improve their lot. They didn't wait for wealth to come to them; they did what was necessary to attract wealth to them. They made things happen rather than wait for things to happen.

STOP READING; TAKE ACTION!

We have one more reason to go before we come to the end of the book, but I would like to ask you to pause right now and mentally review all the information you have picked up so far. Do you feel desire and passion welling up on the inside of you?

At one of my seminars a participant asked me to stop talking because he had heard enough and wanted to go out and take action right there and then. Do you feel like doing that right now?

If you feel like that, you have my permission to put the book down right now and take those first steps you know are necessary for becoming your own boss. I won't be offended that you don't finish reading my book. I will in fact be proud of you for acting on the information.

I will be satisfied with the knowledge that the words I have written in this book inspired somebody like you to get up and set up a business that massively improves your livelihood. I will feel greatly honored to have played a part in your living a better life.

But if you want to finish the book, you are most welcome too. Keep reading right to the end.

LEAVE AN INHERITANCE FOR POSTERITY

L ET ME RELATE to you two stories. They are true stories except for the names. If the names and the stories sound familiar to you, it is coincidental.

THE JOE FAMILY STORY

The first is the story of a senior public servant whom we will call Joe. Joe purchased a house under a Government-sponsored housing scheme. He put up savings with the then Public Officers' Superannuation Fund (POSF, now Nambawan Super) as his equity to borrow money from a bank to buy the house. Over the next 20 years he repaid the bank through salary deductions until he paid back all the money he had borrowed plus interest.

Soon after Joe completed repaying the loan, he reached retirement age and came off the payroll. He did not have much in his bank account because his money habits had been bad. He had wasted a lot of his pay on alcohol and gambling (horse race followed by poker machines when these were introduced in the 1990s), even though he was a responsible father of four children who always made sure that his family had food on the table and paid school fees for the children.

When he left work, the Government gave him a "golden handshake," meaning that he was paid a handsome amount for his services to the country. By this time he was quite old, and his children were grown up. All of them had been to school but none of them had been successful so they were living with the parents.

Joe realized that he had to act quickly to set up something for his children so he purchased a 30-seater truck with cash to operate a passenger ferrying service. He recruited an experienced driver and his two sons took turns in collecting the passengers' fares. He still continued his habit of drinking with his old mates and visiting the pokies parlors on a regular basis.

A few months later, the driver crashed the vehicle. Luckily no one was hurt but the vehicle was damaged beyond repair. Joe and the family were completely devastated because their only means of survival was gone. Joe had not taken comprehensive insurance on the vehicle.

A mechanic had a look at the damaged vehicle and advised that Joe could do two things with it: He could spend a lot of money to bring it back to operation, or he could wreck it and sell the parts to recoup some money. Joe decided he would take the second option simply because he did not have the money to fix the truck.

He made some money by selling parts but it was not enough to sustain the family. To make matters worse, the sons began to associate with wrong company and began drinking as well and bringing young women to the house.

Soon after Joe became ill and after a short time in the hospital, he passed away. The only thing he left to his children and the old woman was the house.

The family continued living together but soon problems began to emerge. The young men brought their girlfriends home and the sisters moved out with their boyfriends. None of them got properly married.

It was not long before the brothers began to quarrel over ownership of the house. The eldest son argued that he should own the place but the younger did not agree. The situation got so tense and interventions by the mother fell on deaf ears.

The mother could not bear it, and died suddenly. Seeing that the mother was out of the way, the eldest son and his de facto wife began to exert more pressure on the younger son and his girlfriend to move out. Fist fights became regular, and in the process furniture, louver glasses and walls were destroyed. Power and water bills were hard to pay so many times services into the property were disconnected.

After a while the brothers came to their senses and decided to sell the house and divide the money equally. Unfortunately the house was quite run-down so they sold it for less than they should have. Their sisters did not get anything from the sale of the house. The brothers spent most of the money on drinking and gambling so now even they don't have anything to live on.

When Joe was working, the family lived well by Papua New Guinea standards. Today, if you were to see the late Joe's children, you wouldn't believe that they grew up in town and enjoyed a better living standard than most other children in the country. They are living in virtual poverty.

THE MATTHEW FAMILY STORY

The second story is that of a young man whom we will call Matthew. He was a highly educated person who had gone overseas for further studies and held a very responsible position with a company. He was married to a woman from his local area and had three beautiful children.

Even though he was highly educated and was professionally successful, he had several weaknesses. He had the habit of drinking with his mates, visiting nightclubs, and womanizing at the back of his wife. Like most working class people, he spent most of what he received, and many times he borrowed money to fund his extravagant lifestyle. When he travelled out of town, he always met up and slept with a woman. The women fell for his good looks and his money and the hired cars he was using.

One night he met a woman in a night club and spent the night with her in the hotel room. Every time he went to this particular night club, he would repeat this habit, sometimes with the same lady and sometimes with others.

A few months later he began to feel weak and tired regularly. He got so worried he decided to go to the hospital for checkup. He got the shock of his life when the blood test result said he was HIV-positive. He arranged for his wife to be tested and she also came out HIV-positive.

Psychologically Matthew and his wife died at that point in time. The thought that they would die leaving three young orphans bothered them so much that their physical conditions deteriorated very fast until they both passed away shortly afterwards.

The children have been adopted by Matthew's older brother James, who has four children of his own. Even though James loves Matthew's children and tries to do his best to be fair with them, the wife often mistreats them.

Matthew didn't leave anything for the children. He actually left them destitute and totally dependent on the goodwill of his family members. The children have not been able to continue going to school due to school fee problems. The dream life they had started to enjoy when their parents were alive has now turned into a painful nightmare.

LESSONS

These are real stories from which we can earn a lot of lessons. In Joe's case, he left something for his children (the house) but it became the subject of contention and friction within the family. It split the family because it was only one house and he had four children. Only the two sons benefited while the daughters missed out completely. His last-ditch efforts to start a business for the family did not work out when the vehicle crashed beyond redemption.

Matthew's story is a very sad one indeed, and I should add that is a story that is being repeated throughout the country. He was a highly-educated person but he did not apply wisdom in how he conducted himself.

Maybe his education got to his head and he thought life was about spending money, drinking and partying. He not only infected his wife with the HIV/AIDS virus which led to her untimely death, but also left three young children as orphans without anything to cater for their future.

IS A JOB AND ITS ENTITLEMENTS REALLY YOURS?

One important point you need to note is that both Joe and Matthew could not pass on their jobs or professions to their children. They only held the jobs as long as they were productive or alive. The moment they passed on, their jobs were taken over by other people.

They were used to thinking that the jobs were theirs. When they conversed with people, they unconsciously referred to the jobs as "my job." Matthew was provided a house and a vehicle by his employer. He would refer to these benefits as "my house" and "my car."

Were the job, house and vehicle really his? No! They belonged to his employer. He enjoyed using them only as long as he was employed. The way the employer allowed him to use these perks made him believe they were his, but when he died, his children could not inherit them. They could not even inherit his job.

CHILDREN CANNOT INHERIT A JOB

So remember this: *Your children cannot inherit your job, nor the perks and privileges that come with it.* You can only pass to your children what you own. If you have a job but do not own anything, there will be nothing for the children to inherit.

Times have really changed, and the majority of people are now part of the cash economy. The days of subsisting off the land are well and truly gone, and money has become essential to life, even in the villages.

Parents now have a greater responsibility to provide for their children's future than ever before. Getting them educated is the minimum they can do for their children.

It is incumbent on parents to go beyond the minimum and set their children up to survive in the new world of the 21st Century – a world of job scarcity, job and financial insecurity, high unemployment, high taxes, rising prices, insufficient superannuation savings, falling health and education standards, no health insurance, marriage and family instability, increased lawlessness and social disharmony as the gap between the 'haves' and the 'have-nots' widens further.

SET UP YOUR CHILDREN
WHILE YOU HAVE A JOB

If you are employed, I want to encourage you to use your pay to set up something for the children. Do not wait until you leave work at retirement. Do not rely on your superannuation savings either. Do not rely on your retirement benefits fund to pass on to your children because sometimes you might not even get that money.

Manage your money wisely. Do something on the side instead of just depending on the pay cheque and letting your employer dictate what you eat, where you go for holidays, what school your children attend, etc. Start a part-time income generating activity.

If you are male and your wife is not employed, set her up to earn something for the family. Use your free time to do something for the family, instead of wasting time and money on useless activities such as watching television, drinking with friends or gambling.

You must leave an inheritance for your children. Many people who had jobs have been cursed by their children because they did not leave a thing for them. When the parents are employed, the children eat all right. But children need something more than food and clothing. *They need an economic foundation to launch out in their generation.*

A GOOD MAN LEAVES AN INHERITANCE TO HIS CHILDREN'S CHILDREN

Being a parent is not only about bringing children into the world, rearing them, getting them educated, etc. It is also about passing something of yourself on to them. It is about living your life through them after you die.

The Bible says this on the subject of inheritance: *"A good man leaves an inheritance for his children's children."* Do you consider yourself to be a good person? One test of you being a good person is that you leave something not only for your children, but also your grandchildren.

THE SELF-EMPLOYED HAVE A BETTER CHANCE OF LEAVING AN INHERITANCE THAN THE EMPLOYED

I am really convinced that self-employment offers the greatest potential for leaving children with something after you depart from this world. Many workers leave nothing for their children. They earn a lot of money and spend it all. They live from payday to payday. Most live beyond their means and support their lifestyles with money borrowed from finance companies and informal money lenders. When they die, there is nothing for their children to start life with. Some even leave debts which their children have to repay.

Working for yourself does not automatically mean you will leave an inheritance for the children. It all depends on your personal money habits. But if you look closely at people who work at a paid job and those who are self-employed, you will realize that business people usually leave more when they pass on than the employed.

SELF-EMPLOYED PEOPLE THINK DIFFERENTLY TO THE EMPLOYED

People who work for others and those who are self-employed think and act differently. Salaried people are always thinking about next pay day so they spend what they have unwisely. Their mentality is, *"Next pay day is always coming."* Their thinking – which they also express verbally – is usually, *"I will save next week."* Or, *"I will do something with my leave pay."*

Most self-employed people never think like that. Their usual mentality is, *"I must use what I have today wisely because there is no guarantee that I will earn something tomorrow."*

They think about how best they can use what they have today. And they usually think about investing rather than spending on consumption. They look for ways to make their money work for them rather than working for money.

OUR ANCESTORS WERE SELF-EMPLOYED

Our ancestors were self-employed. They were their own bosses! They worked when they wanted to, not because they had bosses looking over them, but because they had to survive.

Some became lazy but those lazy ones slept with empty stomachs and did not have anything to contribute towards community activities. Most however were hard workers. They knew how to manage their time wisely. They did not have a concept of saving but their investments were the time and effort they expended in developing their land. They made gardens and planted trees for building houses and fruit trees for food.

Working for someone for a fortnightly salary was a foreign concept to our ancestors. In other countries, only slaves worked for their masters. Their pay was part of what they harvested from working their masters' fields. Others were peasants who worked the royal lands from which they kept the kings' households fed and clothed, after which they fed themselves. They did not own any land.

In our country, where everybody had a piece of land, anybody who slaved for another was *looked down upon* and ridiculed. He became the subject of gossip.

This is in complete contrast to today, where people who have a job (i.e. who work or slave for others) are *looked up to*, and those who try to do something for themselves are belittled and mocked to the point where university graduates are not willing to be engaged in the informal sector out of shame and embarrassment.

LEAVING AN INHERITANCE WAS FOREMOST ON OUR ANCESTORS' MINDS

Think back to how our ancestors lived. Leaving an inheritance was foremost on their minds. They always made sure that they passed on something to their children, especially the sons. They defended their own land and even invaded other territory because they were concerned about their children's future.

If you own land in your village, you must be thankful to your forefathers who fought and defended it with you in mind. Now it is your turn to pass on something to the next generation.

Of course I am not suggesting that you start a tribal war as your ancestors did in order to leave an inheritance for the generations that come out of you. But I am suggesting that you need to learn from the mindset of your ancestors and build a business or invest in other assets which you can pass onto your descendants.

WE LEAVE OUR HABITS WITH OUR CHILDREN

If you link what I have shared in this Chapter with the rest of the book, you will realize that being self-employed will enable you to leave your immediate children as well as future generations with something to start their lives.

Some of the important inheritances you will leave are not physical things like money and houses but your beliefs, values, and habits.

Children learn more by observation than by what they hear. If you are self-employed, you will save and generally use your money more prudently. Indirectly you will be teaching your children prudence when it comes to managing money.

Children will also learn about employing people and leveraging the employees' time and skills. They will learn concepts such as tax, interest, bank reconciliations, customer relations etc. They will be more financially literate than the children of those who work for a pay cheque.

If you work for a salary all your life, you are indirectly teaching your children to do likewise too. You are limiting your childrens' minds to making a living from a fortnightly salary only. When you live from payday to payday, you are teaching your children to do likewise. In fact you will insist that they follow your footsteps.

If you borrow money constantly like the majority of working people do today, you are indirectly teaching your children to do the same when they need money. The result will be that they become habitual borrowers when they grow up.

They will think that it is okay for them to run to the bank or money lenders every time they face financial problems. They will mismanage their money with the knowledge that they can always borrow when they have needs, because that is how they have witnessed you managing your money.

An Australian friend of mine – the person who encouraged me the get into the seminar business – related to me that his father who was a working class person all his life, told my friend that he should not go into business. The father's reasoning was that his grandfather and great grandfather were workers and he himself was a working class person. So he expected his children to be like him. He told my friend, *"We have always been a working class family."*

My friend related that he chose not to just work for a salary. Instead, he decided to start a business and invest in real estate while getting and holding a paid job. His brother followed their father's advice by simply being a working class person. The friend told me that his elder brother was financially weak and highly indebted whereas as he himself had many investments and was financially secure.

He was happy that he did not take his father's advice to be just a working class person. He still had his job, not because he needed money but because the job gave him the opportunity to see different places and meet people at his employer's cost.

CHILDREN OF THE SELF-EMPLOYED THINK FINANCIAL SECURITY WHILE CHILDREN OF EMPLOYEES THINK JOB SECURITY

It is generally true that children of self-employed people usually think about being in business when they grow up, while those of people who work for a salary think about getting paid jobs. The children of the self-employed may get jobs initially but their ultimate dream is to run their own businesses like they see their parents doing.

Children of people who work for others look forward to getting jobs which they can hold for life. This is again because children learn by observation, and usually they aspire to be like their parents.

To put it simply: The children of self-employed people generally seek *financial security* while those of employed people seek *job security*.

I think you will agree that times have become more uncertain for our children than ever before. Jobs have become scarce and there is no safety and security in existing jobs. The whole world has become a "global village" where cash plays a dominant role in the lives of people. The challenge for parents is to conduct their lives in ways that they leave something of their possessions for their children to start their lives with.

Children cannot inherit jobs and professions but they can inherit businesses, investments, habits and legacies. Generally, business people position themselves to bless their children and future generations with assets they have created in their lives.

Those who are dependent on their employers' pay cheques all their working lives generally don't leave much. In fact, the majority of them don't leave anything for their children while some leave unsettled debts which become burdens for their children.

In a society such as we have in Papua New Guinea, people hold families, tribes and communities responsible for the actions of individuals. For instance, somebody accidently kills someone else and the whole tribe carries the burden of reprisals, threats, compensation payments etc.

Likewise, a father dies before repaying his debts and the burden falls immediately on the sons or other family members. I have been in funerals where debtors have come not to mourn for the dead but to inform family members of debts owed to them by the deceased. I have also witnessed family members of dead people repaying debts at the close of funeral ceremonies.

I believe that you are a good person. You will not only leave this world debt-free. But you will also leave something for your children and their children.

Best-selling author and real estate investor Robert T. Kiyosaki has made this statement:

> It is not how much money you make that is important, but how much money you keep [from what you make], how hard it works for you, and how many generations you keep it for.

He is talking about making money work for you by investing it, and leaving an inheritance for your children and their children. How much you make and spend in your lifetime is not important; what is important is how much of that money you leave for future generations.

I submit to you that you have a greater chance of leaving an inheritance for future generations by working for yourself than for someone else. You have a better chance of leaving a tangible inheritance by owning a business. You have a better chance of leaving a strong financial foundation for your children by being in business.

CONCLUSION

ARE YOU PERSUADED, CONVINCED AND INSPIRED?

Just to recap for your convenience, here are the thirty reasons as to why you should think seriously about becoming self-employed and minding your own business:

Reason # 1: Jobs are scarce. If you have just left school or have been looking for a job for some time, there is a high likelihood that you might never get a paid job.

Reason # 2: With the many changes taking place in the world, paid jobs are no longer safe and secure. If you are employed, your job is not safe and secure, even if it seems to be so. Any sense of security you feel is deceptive and false.

Reason # 3: When you get into business, you will have the opportunity to create and have several income types rather than being limited to "earned income."

Reason # 4: When you work for others, you will have only one income source – the fortnightly salary. When you work for yourself, you can have multiple streams of income.

Reason # 5: When you work for a salary, the amount of money you earn in a year is limited. When you become self-employed, your earning capacity and potential will be unlimited.

Reason # 6: You have a better chance of becoming financially independent and free being self-employed than working for an employer. In fact you will never be financially free working for others.

Reason # 7: You gain control over your time, which, in addition to your mind, is your greatest asset. When you work for others, you sell your time and life. You will be ruled and controlled.

Reason # 8: You gain control over your income, tax and your life when you are in business. You determine how much you earn, when you pay tax, and where you want to live.

Reason # 9: A business enables you to get ahead in life by leveraging other peoples' time, strength, knowledge and skills. Needless to say, when you are employed, the employer leverages your time and skills to move forward financially.

Reason # 10: You will contribute to addressing the country's unemployment problem. You will become a part of the solution, not the problem.

Reason # 11: You will develop better money habits as a self-employed person.

Reason # 12: You will make money work for you using systems and other people rather than you working for money by trading your strength and time.

Reason # 13: You will become cost-conscious and profit-minded.

Reason # 14: You will realise your potential more than if you are employed.

Reason # 15: You are a survivor. Self-employment will help you develop the natural 'survivor's instinct' you have been born with.

Reason # 16: You will be better able to protect your assets through a company than as an individual.

Reason # 17: You will enjoy tax advantages which are available for those who operate in the informal sector.

Reason # 18: You will benefit from tax advantages which are available to people who own companies.

Reason # 19: A business can help you to avoid poverty of the working class.

Reason # 20: Self-employment gives you the potential to become a more generous person.

Reason # 21: You may or may not go to business school but no school can ever teach the kind of education you receive as a self-employed person.

Reason # 22: Self-employment provides you the opportunity to gain a lot of new knowledge.

Reason # 23: You will also gain new skills, including people skills, marketing skills, financial skills, etc.

Reason # 24: Competition is stiff in the business world. As you get into business for yourself, market forces will shape, mould and sharpen you such that you become alert and competitive.

Reason # 25: When you are employed, you become 'entitlement' minded. You become free of depending on others when you become self-employed.

Reason # 26: What you earn from working will never be adequate for you to retire on. When you become your own boss, you can retire while you are still young and strong.

Reason # 27: When you work for others, you will not be paid enough to send your children to good schools. But you can give them a better education by owning a business.

Reason # 28: Inflation sets all working class people back. You can beat inflation and even ride on it through your own business.

Reason # 29: Building a business is like building your own pipeline into the economy. You will have access to more of the money that is flowing in the economy than salaried people.

Reason # 30: You cannot pass on your job to your children, but they can inherit your business and investments.

THE SOLUTION TO UNEMPLOYMENT IS NOT EMPLOYMENT BUT SELF-EMPLOYMENT

I have literally cracked my head and scrubbed my heart to put this book together because I am convinced that self-employment holds the answer to our country's unemployment problem. No matter how many jobs the Government and large investors create, there will always be a large number of educated but unemployed people.

The Papua New Guinea Government aims to facilitate the establishment of 500,000 new locally-owned businesses by the year 2030 under its Small and Medium Enterprise (SME) Policy. These business – if set up and operated successfully – are expected to employ an average of four people each. The total number of new jobs anticipated to be created is two million.

But the total population is projected to rise to eleven million by 2030. The implication is that even if the number of jobs rise by that much, there will still be too many people looking for jobs.

Unemployed people are very frustrated because the education system has promised them a world which does not existent. People have invested a lot of time and money on getting educated with the hope of getting jobs but the reality is that there are not enough jobs around. It is like driving up a dead-end road.

So a lot of young people are venting their frustrations on society through all kinds of anti-social behaviour. As long as there are not enough jobs for people to earn their living from, lawlessness will thrive and set the country back.

One of my visions is therefore to give hope to these hopeless people both directly and indirectly. My belief is actually that the majority of people leaving school in Papua New Guinea do not really need paid jobs to survive. What they need is help with ideas, inspiration, motivation, and guidance to start their own businesses.

SALARIED PEOPLE CAN BE LOOKED DOWN ON

I look forward to the day when people look down on those who work at salaried jobs and up to business people. I look forward to the day when only the lazy look for paid jobs while the majority of able-bodied people start their own businesses immediately upon graduating from school.

I believe that this can happen. Papua New Guineans have land, which is one of the most important factors of production.

Every body that has land can become self-employed and go on to living an enviable life.

I hope to get people thinking like this: *"Let people who need jobs look for them. I would rather work for myself than allow myself to be used to make others rich at my expense."*

I have been self-employed since 2001. My mind-set has changed completely. Whereas previously I thought having a job was enviable, today I pity those who work for others. I see them rushing off to work every morning and I feel sorry for them.

I know that a lot of these people do not earn enough from their jobs with the result that they are just keeping their heads above water financially. Many are actually up to their necks in debt. Most are running the 'financial rat race' without realizing it. They are jogging on 'financial treadmills' without getting anywhere. They are really rushing off every morning to 'nowhere.'

I know that if they cared to look at how the money they earn is flowing in their lives, they would realise that they are working for the Government, their debtors and providers of goods and services more than for themselves.

I also know that they could be much better off using their time, skills and expertise for themselves. So I pity them and I know that all self-employed people pity those who work for others too.

DIFFERENCES BETWEEN THE EMPLOYED AND THE SELF-EMPLOYED

Throughout the two books I have attempted to highlight some of the major differences between people who are employed and people who are self-employed.

I really hope that I have persuaded, convinced and motivated you to start thinking about and taking steps towards being your own boss. You owe it to yourself, your children and the wider community to do so, because I have not given you five, ten, fifteen or even twenty reasons. I have given you thirty reasons in the two volumes! And if you think deeply enough, you might come up with additional reasons as to why you should mind your own business.

I have related how I vowed in 2001 to never work for a fortnightly salary again. When I made that decision, I did not know all that I have related in this book. If I had read such a book back then, I might have made the decision much earlier.

You are at an advantage now that you have read the books compared to when I set out to work for myself. If I had not been forced to a corner as I was then, it is probable that I would never have become self-employed. Getting sacked has been the most defining moment in my life. It has changed the course of our lives as a family.

I hope that reading *Be Your Own Boss!* has become a destiny-defining experience. As I have related at the beginning of this volume, many people have testified to starting their own businesses after reading Volume 1. Some have told me that they were seriously thinking about it. So the book has inspired many readers. I hope it has inspired you too.

I plan to write a book in the future re-telling all the real-life stories my readers share with me. I know that that book will be even more inspiring. Maybe yours will be one of the stories that are featured in that book. When you do become your own boss, please let me know. I also need to be motivated by your feedback to keep on motivating other people.

I AM NOT ANTI-EMPLOYMENT

As we draw towards the close of this two-volume book discussing why you should become self-employed, I must make this qualification: *I am not anti-employment.* My purpose in writing this book is not to discourage you from looking for or getting a job. And it is certainly not to encourage you to resign from your job.

My sole purpose has been to show you that there is another world – the world of self-employment and business – which you may not have thought about because of getting indoctrinated in school that the only way to live a good life is by getting a paid job.

My real target groups are students and unemployed people which number in the hundreds of thousands today. I aim to encourage them to consider the possibility of getting into business for themselves when job-hunting proves to be fruitless. Instead of feeling hopeless and frustrated they should know that self-employment is a viable option.

So if you are currently employed and feel compelled to leave your job to start your own business after reading the book, you would effectively be intercepting a message I have meant for another audience.

THERE CERTAINLY ARE ADVANTAGES
OF HOLDING A PAID JOB

Now that I have discussed many reasons for having a business and becoming your own boss, let me say that there are also advantages in getting a job and becoming somebody else's employee. Several of the obvious advantages are:

1. A job promises a fixed yet regular income which provides more security than a business.

2. If you manage your pay well, you will have seed-money to invest in a business. Many people have good business ideas but don't have the money to put their ideas into practice. Having a job is a definite advantage as it can be a source of seed capital.

3. If you hold a senior position, some personal expenses such as school fees, rent and car expenses, are met by the employer. When you become self-employed, you lose because you have to pay all these expenses yourself.

4. Most employers provide personal accident insurance while some provide medical and even life insurance. Most self-employed people don't have any insurance at all.

5. Your employers contribute to retirement savings. The majority of self-employed people don't have anything to fall back on when their businesses fail.

6. You can receive further education at the employers' expense, both more advanced studies and short-term courses. Self-employed people rarely have the time to further their education in institutions, and those who do have to pay out of their own pockets.

7. A paid job provides the opportunity for you to establish contacts and gain experience and skills which can stand you in good stead later in your own business.

8. You can travel to many places at the employers' expense, both within the country and overseas.

9. You get looked up to and respected by your family and the community at large because you have a job, even if you are not highly paid. This boosts your moral and sense of worth.

I am sure that you can think of several more advantages which I have not listed here. Having a job can be satisfying.

But I suggest to you that the advantages of self-employment far outweigh the benefits you realise from having a job. The benefits of being employed are also temporary or short-term in duration. You lose them when you lose the job; you certainly lose them when you retire.

THE QUESTION IS NOT *WHETHER*, BUT *WHEN*

As I have pointed out to you, your ancestors were self-employed. Everyone was their own boss. Most people lived in relative affluence then.

I have also reminded you that the day is coming when you have to leave your job whether you like it or not. When that day arrives, you will inevitably go back to being self-employed because your superannuation fund savings will not be sufficient for you to maintain your pre-retirement standard of living.

So the question really is not *whether* you should start working for yourself, but *when*. I guess an alternative question can be, "*If not now, when?*"

I have attempted to persuade you that the sooner you start thinking about minding your own business and becoming your own boss, the better for you, your family, your community, and your country.

I hope that I have succeeded in convincing you. I trust that you are persuaded, convinced beyond any doubt, inspired, and motivated. I hope that you feel blown up on the inside like a balloon, filled to the brim with inspiration and fired up in your belly, so much so that you cannot wait to establish your very own private money pipeline.

WITHOUT A STRONG ENOUGH *WHY,* EVEN THE EASIEST *HOW* WILL BE TOO HARD

This may be the first such book you have read. You may be wondering why I have devoted a whole book discussing the reasons for starting or owing your own business.

My answer is firstly that starting and operating a business is not easy. It takes a lot of time, guts, and money. Secondly, most aspiring business people give up when they face difficulties and hardships in the process of starting their businesses. They get all psyched up about having their own business but turn cold when they are confronted by the first obstacle or setback.

Evidence all over the world demonstrates that more than 90% of businesses do not survive the first year of existence. There are many reasons for this (such as improper research and planning, inadequate finance, cash flow problems, bad location, bad business partners, mismanagement, etc.), but one which I have addressed in this book is motivation on the part of the would-be business person.

You see, becoming successful has a lot to do with what you feel on the inside of you. Difficulties will come, but if you are highly motivated and determined, you will go through those difficulties, not balk at them and throw in the towel.

I could have started with a book on how to start a business but I chose to focus on the reasons first because I am convinced that without a strong enough *why*, even the easiest *how* will be too hard. That is to say, unless you have one or several compelling reasons for doing something, you won't gather up the self-confidence and the will to do it even if you are shown the easiest way of doing that thing.

Most people fail in life because they want to do things without convincing themselves of the benefits they will realize for taking action. They start out with gusto but run out of steam along the way because they don't have enough good reasons to persist until they succeed. They lose 'staying power.'

So my objective for providing the reasons for starting a business first has been to build you up on the inside so that you will keep on running the course despite the hardships and roadblocks you are definitely going to be faced with in pursuing your dream of becoming a business owner and attaining financial independence and freedom.

I read a statement once which has stuck with me, and it goes like this: *"He who has a why to live for can bear almost any how."*

It means that when a person has one or several motivating reasons for doing something, that person will accomplish the task despite the hardships they face. If you place a road block in their path, they will drive right through it if they cannot find an alternative route. Why? *Because they have a reason or compelling motive for getting to the other side.*

They tell themselves that they must get to their destination – *no matter what.* They have such a burning desire to reach their goal that no obstacle can knock them back. What drives them to persist in spite of the hindrances, difficulties and setbacks along the way is the benefit they hope to receive or enjoy at the end of the journey.

That is the kind of attitude I wanted to develop in you. I wanted to bring you to a point in your thinking where you tell yourself, *"I am going to start a business – no matter what, and come what may."* I hope that I have succeeded.

GET THE SPIRIT OF THE BOOK

In closing, let me encourage you to read the book several times. Reading just once may not be enough for the information to sink into your subconscious mind. In fact I would urge you to go a step further and *study* both volumes of *Be Your Own Boss. Get the spirit of the books, not just the letter.*

I would also encourage you to share the information with friends and acquaintances. Don't be secretive with information and ideas. Share freely because the more you do that, the more you will receive new ideas. In fact, the more you talk to people about what you have learnt from the book, the more convinced you will become to go out and start your own business.

Not only that. You will find that your mind becomes clearer when you speak things out. When you talk to people, you will make finer distinctions in your own mind. You will become even more inspired and convinced by listening to yourself talk about it. You will definitely learn more than you have read from the book when you discuss with others. As the saying goes, *"Teaching teaches the teacher."*

I wish you well as you ponder becoming your own boss. I am really hopeful that you will join me and many others as your own boss soon.

www.ingramcontent.com/pod-product-compliance
Lightning Source LLC
Chambersburg PA
CBHW021412210526
45463CB00001B/326